WITCHCRAFT

WITCHCRAFT

GEDDES & GROSSET

Published by Geddes & Grosset, an imprint of
Children's Leisure Products Limited

© 2000 Children's Leisure Products Limited, David Dale House,
New Lanark, ML11 9DJ, Scotland

First published 2000

ISBN 1 85534 354 1

Printed and bound in the UK

Contents

Chapter 1

Introduction

From childhood we all have a clear, preconceived idea of what a witch looks like – an ugly old woman wearing a black cloak and a tall, pointed, wide-brimmed hat, who gets around by flying through the air on a broomstick and who is frequently to be found cackling wickedly while stirring some foul-smelling brew in a black cauldron or casting evil spells. The picture is often extended to include a black cat that goes everywhere with her and a tumbledown cottage.

Unfortunately the clarity of our perception of the traditional witch does not extend to witchcraft. We know that it is traditionally associated with magic and sorcery but, after that, vagueness sets in. This is perfectly understandable as the word has been used to describe different concepts at different points in history.

Margaret Murray and the Pagan Theory

The confusion over the exact nature of witchcraft was far from helped by the writings of Margaret Murray, a British anthropologist, archaeologist and Egyptologist, who was born in 1863 and died in 1963, and who became interested in witchcraft in the course of her study of Egyptology. It was her contention, as set out in her book, *The Witch-cult in Western Europe*, published in 1921, that the history of witchcraft was an ongoing one, that witchcraft was originally an old pagan, organized religion dating back to earliest times and that the witchcraft which was the centre of so much hysteria in the Middle Ages and the Renaissance was a remnant of this ancient religion.

Some of Murray's conclusions were based on *The Golden Bough*, written by Sir James Frazer and published in 1890, in which the author raised the question of witchcraft having Palaeolithic origins. Murray, however, took the matter much further and maintained that there was a strong connection between what was known about some of the early pagan religious practices and the rites that were described by those confessing to witchcraft during the period of witchcraft hysteria, part of her research having included written records of witchcraft trials. According to her way of thinking, the supposed old religion of witchcraft had been alive, in part, all the time but had been driven underground by Christianity. The theory was that the old rituals had survived because of the meetings of a series of covens throughout the ages.

Murray's suggestion that witchcraft represents a continuing and continuous pagan religion was the subject of much controversy. Her theory is upheld by many modern witches but much of it has been rejected by modern scholars on the grounds of lack of evidence. She did not do her credibility much good by the publication of *The Divine King* in England in 1954 in which she contended that from William the Conqueror on every English king as far as James I and VI was a closet witch and also alleged that over the centuries many statesmen had been killed by witch's ritual rather than by the presumed means.

Murray's theories of witchcraft as an unbroken, secret, pagan religion that had suddenly become more prominent and more public during periods noted for their witchcraft hysteria did not take into account the part that the Church played in this hysteria. Nor did it place enough emphasis on the fact that the confessions that were a major part of the basis of her research were completely contrived. A great many such confessions were extracted by some form of enforced distress, whether this took the form of excruciating torture by some terrible device or some more subtle form, and the similarity that was a feature of these even from country to country was largely because of the degree of standardization of the questions. The similarity in witchcraft trials in different countries was far greater than might be supposed because of the existence of *Malleus Maleficarum*, a book on witchcraft first published in Germany in 1486 and known as the 'Hammer of the Witches', a kind of guidebook to witchcraft and the prosecution of witches, which was adopted as a kind of guidebook for witchcraft trials throughout Europe and later England.

Inquisition

The role that the Church played in the supposed rise of witchcraft is an important one. This role was an extension of its role as an exterminator of heretics. The Roman Catholic Church's vigorous campaign to stamp out heresy in Christian parts of the world began early in the thirteenth century. It was part of this campaign to establish tribunals, known as the Inquisition, an institution that acquired and has retained throughout history a reputation for the use of great cruelty and torture in pursuit of its aims to identify all heretics and to punish them, often by death and often by burning to death.

Before the Church courts, and the Inquisition in particular, turned their attention towards witchcraft there had been people accused of being involved in magic of various kinds. An interest in magic and sorcery has been part of sections of most societies from earliest times. However, an association with magic was not thought to be among the more heinous of crimes, being usually punished by fines or imprisonment.

Canon Episcopi

The problem for witchcraft was that it became designated as a form of heresy and former attitudes changed dramatically. It might confidently have been assumed that witchcraft was safe from such charges because there was in existence an important and respected religious document of unknown origin and uncertain date, called *Canon Episcopi*, that stated that witchcraft was a delusion and a belief in it the act of an infidel. This had been incorporated into canon law around the middle of the twelfth century. Thus it was thought at this time that it was not witchcraft that was heresy, since this was simply the result of a fevered imagination, but belief in such a thing.

Although the *Canon Episcopi* denied the existence of witchcraft it unwittingly helped to promote the movement against it. It referred to deluded women who thought that they had the ability to ride on animals to night-time services dedicated to their mistress, the pagan goddess Diana, and some of the imagined activities of witches described in the Canon were part of the basis of future charges against accused witches.

The *Canon Episcopi* was a much respected document for a long time but gradually attitudes to witchcraft changed. The views of the Dominican theologian Thomas Aquinas (1226–74) did much to foster the Church's change in attitude. It was his belief that, among other things, witches could fly through the air, change shape, raise storms, have implicit pacts with the devil and have sexual intercourse with demons. It was also part of his belief that demons and the devil tempt people.

Witchcraft as Heresy

Aquinas was an important figure in theology and much attention was paid to his views. These were to have a great effect on the thinking of those involved in the later prosecution of witches and they markedly influenced the Church's views on witchcraft.

There remained the matter of the *Canon Episcopi*, but ways around this were sought and it began to be discredited. There was a gradual but marked move to label witchcraft as both a reality and a form of heresy, and many people were prosecuted and burnt as witches in southern France in the first part of the fourteenth century, such action also spreading to Italy, Germany and Switzerland

These anti-witchcraft activities were given a tremendous boost in 1484 when Pope Innocent VIII issued a papal bull that emphasized the importance of the Inquisition and its zeal against heretics, referred to wicked acts being carried out in northern Germany and elsewhere, and condemned the people allegedly performing such acts as blasphemously renouncing their faith. The acts referred to included consorting with demons and using spells to bring harm to people, crops or animals.

Members of the Inquisition were delighted by the papal

action, which meant that they could officially view witchcraft as a form of heresy and treat accused witches in the same way that they treated accused heretics. In any case, they were running out of heretics, so many people having been accused and burned to death by this time. Two years later was published the *Malleus Maleficarum* (*see* page 15 and Chapter 4, page 266), compiled by two Dominican members of the Inquisition, known as the Hammer of the Witches, a kind of guidebook to witchcraft and the prosecution of witches, which was to have a powerful influence on those who identified accused witches and prosecuted and sentenced them.

Thus began the spate of witchcraft trials described in Chapter 2 and based on the methods already established by the Inquisition in heresy trials. Because of the supposed connection between witchcraft and heresy, a great number of people were submitted to extreme torture and lost their lives. Witchcraft hysteria was at its peak between 1560 and 1660, although it lasted to a lesser degree for about another ninety years. At the height of the Inquisition witchcraft trials, the worst persecution took place in France and in Germany.

The Inquisition itself was responsible for few of the trials after 1500, later trials being conducted either by other ecclesiastical courts or secular ones. By the 1730s the persecution of accused witches, whether by the church or by the state, had largely reached an end in Europe, Britain and America. However, the last executions on the grounds of witchcraft did not take place in France until 1745, and in Bavaria Anna Maria Schwagel was the last person to be executed for witchcraft – she was beheaded.

Witchcraft in England

It has to be remembered that the Inquisition's activities against accused witches were confined to continental Europe. The torture that was seen as a necessary part of the trials was banned in England and witchcraft was regarded as a civil crime. In addition, the *Malleus Maleficarum* was not translated into English until 1584, and so it exerted an influence on witchcraft trials that happened nearly a hundred years after it had been compiled. In England execution for witchcraft was by hanging not burning.

In England witchcraft hysteria did not come into its own until much later than it did in continental Europe. There was an act passed by Henry VIII in 1542 that allowed for accused witches to be tried and punished by the state, but the aim of this Witchcraft Act was to prevent supposed witches from inflicting harm on others, not to have them tried for heresy. In fact this law brought the trial of only one person and even this resulted in a pardon, and the act was repealed in 1547 by Edward VI.

In 1563, however, Queen Elizabeth passed another Witchcraft Act that was to mark the beginning of witchcraft hysteria in England. Although the tenets of the act were not as severe as the legislation in Europe, they did allow for the death penalty for those found guilty of murder by witchcraft or sorcery. It is thought that Elizabeth was much influenced by some of her bishops, who had witnessed some of the European trials and consequent burnings, and by the fact that there were rumours of witchcraft plots against herself. In addition, fears about witchcraft were affecting the general public, rumours about what was happening on the Continent having reached England. Thus, although witchcraft hysteria in England had nothing directly to do with charges of heresy it did indirectly, news of the European trials having brought fear and unrest about the potential presence of witchcraft.

Another more stringent act was passed in 1581, but it was nothing like as stringent as the Witchcraft Act passed by James I of England (and VI of Scotland) in 1604. Many of the most important English witchcraft trials were conducted under the terms of this act. It allowed for the execution by hanging of anyone found guilty of trying to cause harm to someone else by means of witchcraft, whether or not the person at the receiving end of the witchcraft had actually died. It also made it a felony to consort with any evil spirits.

The worst of the English witchcraft hysteria occurred in the 1640s, when the country was in the grip of political and social unrest and in a mood to look for scapegoats. This was the period during which the notorious witch-finder Matthew Hopkins operated (*see* Chapter 2, page 58). The 1604 act remained in force until 1736. In the latter half of the seventeenth century the witchcraft hysteria gradually tapered off. The last person to be executed on charges of witchcraft in England was Alice Molland in Exeter in 1684. The last person to have a serious indictment brought against her was Jane Clarke in Leicester in 1717 but the case was thrown out of court, despite the large number of people wishing to testify against her.

There was much more of an archetypal witch in England than in Europe. There was more variation in the nature of the suspect in Europe, and it was the case with some European courts that they set their sights on the wealthy, since people convicted of witchcraft had to pay for their own trials and executions and had any remaining estate confiscated. In England the typical accused witch was a strange-looking, solitary elderly woman of eccentric habits and low social standing, who kept a cat. Such people were easy to intimidate and few would bother to come to their aid. There were, of course, exceptions to the rule.

Witchcraft in Scotland

In Scotland accused witches were treated much more brutally than they were in England. Indeed, their treatment was on a par with many of the European countries. Although the Inquisition was not involved, many of their methods were and the Presbyterian Church, as well as the secular courts, exhibited a zeal to stamp out witchcraft.

Witchcraft hysteria took some time to reach Scotland but when it did it was exceptionally strong. As was the case with England, the Inquisition with its charges of heresy was not the direct cause of the witchcraft trials in Scotland but it was an indirect cause since what was happening in Europe affected Scotland even more than it did England, Scotland's European links then being the stronger. A fear of witchcraft was therefore communicated to the people of Scotland.

Mary Queen of Scots in 1563 introduced tougher legislation against witchcraft than had formerly been the case. However, it was not until the coming to the throne of James VI, who was later also to become James I of England, that witchcraft hysteria in Scotland came into its own. He has been blamed for having added much fuel to the fire of this hysteria but it has been claimed that this was an unfair accusation and he was simply a product of his times as far as witchcraft was concerned, his views simply reflecting the prevalent views of the day.

However, James did have much contact with the Continent and was aware of the attitude to witchcraft there and of the trials that were going on. He was apparently originally sceptical of the confessions of some of the witches in the North Berwick Witchcraft Trials in 1590 (*see* Chapter 2, page 38), but his interest in witchcraft grew and his studies on the subject led to a book on the subject being written by him. Entitled *Daemonologie*, it appeared in 1597 and is claimed, at the very least, to have brought attention to and reinforced the then prevailing attitude to witchcraft and, at worst, to have fanned the flames of witchcraft hysteria among the general public. By 1604 James was also king of England and the act that was passed there (*see* Witchcraft in England, page 19) was also valid in Scotland. It is said that, despite his interest in the subject, his belief in many of the alleged acts of witchcraft and his defence of the test of swimming (*see* Chapter 2, page 77), he tried to calm some of the hysteria when it grew excessive.

Witchcraft trials in Scotland were notorious for the use of barbaric forms of torture that were banned in England. These included the use of devices of torture, such as thumbscrews (known in Scotland as pilliwinks) and boots as well as more subtle forms of torture such as sleep deprivation (*see* Chapter 2, page 82). Scotland was more like Europe in its manner of execution and convicted witches were burnt.

After around the year 1700 the number of witchcraft trials tapered off. The last actual trial specifically on the grounds of witchcraft took place in June 1727 when Janet Horne was convicted and put to death in Dornoch. The manner of her death illustrates the brutality of the Scottish witchcraft proceedings. She was placed in a burning barrel of pitch.

Witchcraft in the American Colonies

Witchcraft hysteria in the American colonies, although Salem (*see* Chapter 2, page 41) has gone down in history because of the hysteria there, never reached anything like the level of intensity that it did elsewhere. Witchcraft trials did not begin in the American colonies until the 1640s, the time when the witch-hunts were reaching their peak in England. As far as attitudes to witchcraft were concerned, the colonies were affected by what was happening in England but to a much lesser extent. Apart from those executed at Salem there are recorded as being around only twelve executions on charges of witchcraft in New England.

Witchcraft in Ireland

Despite its long connection with legends of the supernatural and its mystic Celtic connections, Ireland remained free of the hysterical attitude to witchcraft that pervaded mainland Europe, England and Scotland. It has been suggested that this was largely owing to the fact that Ireland was more inaccessible from mainland Europe than were Scotland and England and had fewer European contacts.

Alice Kyteler

The first recorded witchcraft trial in Ireland took place in 1324. It concerned a rich aristocratic woman, Alice Kyteler, who lived in Kilkenny and had amassed a great deal of wealth on the death of her three husbands. When her fourth husband, Sir John Le Poer, was taken ill, he and his children, who did not want their father's money to go to Alice, suggested to the local Franciscan bishop, Richard de Ledre, that Poer's illness was attributable to Alice and possibly to witchcraft.

The bishop, who may well have encountered the European stance on witchcraft during his years of religious training in France and who probably had a view to confiscating Alice's estate should she be found guilty, agreed with the suspicions of the family. Alice was accused among other things of consorting with a demon, holding sacrilegious services, leading a group of devil-worshippers and murdering her first three husbands.

Alice Kyteler had powerful friends, and the bishop had the disadvantage in Ireland of being English-born. He had great difficulty in bringing charges against her and when he eventually succeeded it was to find that she had escaped to England. In her absence she was found guilty of witchcraft and heresy but she lived out the rest of her life in England.

Unfortunately some of those accused of being associated in witchcraft with Kyteler were not so lucky. Her maid, Petronilla, was flogged senseless repeatedly until she confessed that the charges against her and Kyteler were true. She was then excommunicated as a heretic and burned alive on charges of witchcraft in November 1324. Some others who had been accused with Kyteler are said to have been found and variously punished, some being executed by burning.

Magee Island Witches

This might have established a pattern in Ireland and been the start of witchcraft hysteria, but this did not prove to be the case. There are records of only a few trials, around eight, taking place between the first, as described above, in 1324 and the last in 1711 (*see* Chapter 3, Magee Island Witches, page 158). A Witchcraft Act was passed in Ireland in 1586 and was not repealed until 1821 but it was not brought into play very often.

Modern Witchcraft

The second part of the twentieth century witnessed a renewal of interest in witchcraft, but it is a different kind witchcraft and is often known as Wicca to differentiate it. Most of the practitioners of modern witchcraft claim that their cult is purely concerned with benevolent magic and reject any connection with its malevolent counterpart. Although modern witchcraft and Satanism are frequently confused, often because of how the former is portrayed in works of literature, plays and films, there is no connection between the two. Unlike Satanism, or alleged traditional witchcraft, modern witches do not claim any kind of alliance with the devil.

Modern witchcraft, or Wicca, is often described as a neo-pagan movement. Some members of the movement have been influenced by the writings of Margaret Murray (*see* page 13), which are described above, and regard their organization as having an continuous link with an early organized pagan witchcraft movement, driven underground by the advent of Christianity. However, Margaret Murray's theories on this have largely been discredited.

Some of the rituals of Wicca are reminiscent of some pagan beliefs and rituals, and it is thought that isolated groups throughout the centuries kept these alive without belonging to an organized witchcraft movement. For example, the object of worship of modern witches is the goddess, sometimes in partnership with her consort, the horned god (*see* Chapter 4, pages 212, 215). Wicca, however, is essentially a modern movement.

Modern witchcraft owes its existence in no small part to Gerald Gardner (*see* Chapter 3, page 132). His writings, which drew on folklore, ancient pagan rites and ceremonial magic, caused many people in Britain to develop an interest in witchcraft. He set up his own coven after the repeal of the witchcraft Act in 1951 and many others followed suit. At the time that Gardner was writing, Murray's theory had not yet been discredited and Gardner claimed to be keeping the old witchcraft cult alive by making it known to potential members.

Interest in modern witchcraft grew stronger throughout the 1960s and 1970s and spread to America, where it generated much activity. Many of the original members were women who were also interested in feminism and so a connection was established between the two. At first what was known as the Gardnerian tradition was followed but then Alexander Sanders founded his own tradition, although it too relied heavily on Gardner's rituals.

There are various traditions in the modern movement, and these are ever evolving and changing. They are essentially autonomous and there is no cohesive structure or central authority. The covens within each tradition are also autonomous, each with its own 'book of shadows' (*see* Chapter 4, page 248), which describes the coven's rituals, rules, etc. The modern witchcraft movement, which is imbued with a great respect for Nature, tends to be rather fragmented and, since many covens regard secrecy as being important, it is difficult to judge the extent of it.

Although modern practitioners of modern witchcraft claim that their practices are entirely harmless, there remains a good deal of suspicion directed at them. The word suggests the practices with which accused witches were charged in the period of witchcraft hysteria in Europe, England and Scotland, and the association remains in the minds of people. Also, Gardner was associated with the performance of ritual sexual acts and, although these are now mostly symbolic rather than actual, an image of witchcraft as an orgiastic movement remains.

Chapter 2

Witchcraft Trials and Executions

Witchcraft was regarded as an extremely serious offence, particularly in Europe, and was treated as a crime that was on a par with heresy. Indeed, in Europe it was often viewed as a type of heresy. Like heresy, it was seen as a crime against God himself since people found guilty of witchcraft were assumed to have made a pact with the devil and to have turned their backs on God. In fact, in the earlier witch trials the proceedings were seen as a matter for the church, and the trial was conducted by the ecclesiastical courts, the secular authorities becoming involved only at the punishment stage. The first secular witchcraft trials were held in Paris in 1390.

In several European countries the heresy trials conducted by the Inquisition were used as models for witchcraft trials. There was therefore very little value placed on proof, people being convicted on supposed voluntary confessions and the flimsiest of circumstantial evidence. It was assumed by the authorities from the start that the accused was guilty and it was just a matter of going through the motions, although these could be very savage indeed.

Little or no help was given to the accused. Witnesses for the defence were often not allowed to enter the courtroom. In fact, there were not many defence witnesses anyhow, since speaking up in defence of an accused witch was likely to result in a charge of witchcraft being made against the speaker. Those witnesses who were called to speak for the prosecution had the right to remain anonymous, a fact that made it very difficult for the accused to reply to their evidence. The accused often had to speak for themselves at their trials since it was common to debar them from having lawyers representing them.

Much emphasis was placed on confession, particularly in the continental courts. Most people who were accused of witchcraft did not lightly confess to this, and the courts resorted to torture to extract admissions from the accused (*see* Tests, Confession and Torture below, page 71). The value placed on confession did much to encourage the witch hysteria that swept Europe, since many of those who were forced to make confessions with regard to their associates simply named anyone who came to mind. Thus people lived in fear of a representative of the authorities calling on them with an accusation of involvement in witchcraft.

The witchcraft trials were a source of terror wherever they were held. Because of the number of people that were named in the supposed voluntary confessions forced out of the accused, the number of people put on trial in any one place could be very substantial indeed. Given the reputation enjoyed by the courts of mainland Europe for almost always obtaining a conviction and therefore an execution, the witchcraft trials frequently resulted in mass slaughter.

Famous European Witchcraft Trials

Bamberg Trials

Of the European witchcraft trials, among the most notorious took place in the German principality of Bamberg. It was under the rule of Bishop Johann Gottfried von Aschhausen, which lasted from 1609 until 1622, that the persecution of people accused of witchcraft began. Between three and four hundred people at least were said to have been executed during this time, but this was nothing compared to what was to come. In 1623 Gottfried Johann Georg II Fuchs von Dornheim, who ruled until 1633, began a reign of terror in the area. He established an extremely efficient and extremely cruel campaign under the supervision of the suffragan bishop, Friedrich Forner, with the aim of eradicating any traces of witchcraft from the state.

Local people were encouraged to inform on each other on the least suspicion of witchcraft, and often this information was based on nothing at all, simply being an act of vengeance or an attempt to turn away attention and charges from the informers themselves. The witch-hunts were extremely thorough, and special prisons had to be built to accommodate the huge numbers of accused witches. Von Dornheim had a vested interest in trying and executing as many people as possible, since the estates of those executed for witchcraft were confiscated and the proceeds given to him after the expenses of the trial, torturing and execution had been deducted.

The most shocking aspect of the Bamberg trials was the use

of the most barbaric and agonising forms of torture. Professional torturers skilled in the art were invited to Bamberg, and they used a wide range of devices in the torturing process, including the use of thumbscrews, boots, the rack and strappado (described below under Torture by Device, page 83). In addition, the accused were immersed in boiling hot baths to which lime had been added, placed upon a roasting hot iron chair, forced to kneel on a spiked board and placed in stocks fitted with iron spikes. There seemed no end to the savagery to which the Bamberg courts would put their victims.

As was usually the case in the European courts, the whole trial system was stacked against the accused persons. They were not allowed to have lawyers represent them and they were often not told the exact nature of the charges against them or the identity of their accusers. It was simply a question of getting them to make a supposed voluntary confession and torturing them until they did so. Even after they were condemned to death, the torture would not be stopped and was continued even while they were on the way to the place of execution.

The great in the land were not even exempt from this reign of terror, probably because von Dornheim had his eye on their wealth, much of which would go to him when they were executed. Anyone who dared to protest, either on behalf of an individual suspect or against the whole terrible process in general, was seized and charged with witchcraft.

Hysteria and panic reigned. People tried to escape but many were intercepted. Help was sought from the Holy Roman Emperor, Ferdinand, but von Dornheim paid no attention to his attempts at intervention and, although Ferdinand issued mandates in 1630 and 1631 banning the persecution, the situation did not really improve until von Dornheim died in 1632.

Trèves Trials

Germany was noted for the extent of its witchcraft hysteria. One area where this was particularly extensive in the late sixteenth century was Trèves, now Trier. The situation was at its worst from 1582 on and was largely instigated by Prince-Bishop Johann von Schonenberg, with the help of Johann Zandt, the governor, a notary, Peter Ormsdorf, and Suffragan Bishop Peter Binsfield.

The reign of terror began with von Schonenberg attacking Dietrich Flade, one of the civil judges who officiated at witchcraft trials, for being too lenient. Flade was tried as a witch and executed, and there began a whole spate of trials. Attempts made by a priest, Cornelious Loos, to bring attention to the lawless trials that were taking place were in vain as the church refused to act and, indeed, banished Loos to Belgium.

Between the years of 1587 and 1594 around six thousand people were accused, and there was general hysteria. Hardly any of the accused escaped torture and many were executed. Of those tried and found guilty, a great many were prominent affluent citizens. As was the case in Bamberg, money was a great motivator when it came to accusing witches because their estates were confiscated by the state after the expenses of their trial, torture and execution had been met.

Würzburg Trials

Germany was infamous for the severity of its witchcraft trials. Some of the worst of these occurred in Würzburg in the early seventeenth century. Between 1623 and 1633, during the rule of Prince Bishop Philip Adolf von Ehrenberg, nearly one thousand witches were executed. This slaughter was largely at the instigation of the Jesuits, and, as was the case in Bamberg and Trèves, many of the people executed were affluent, thus swelling the state coffers and those of the Jesuits when their estates were confiscated.

There was widespread hysteria and terror, and the situation was changed only when von Ehrenberg's heir, Ernest Ehrenberg, was suddenly seized, subjected to a secret trial for involvement with witchcraft and summarily executed. The Prince Bishop, who had not been informed, seems to have come to his senses at this point, although up until then he had gone along with the evil work of the Jesuits. He became more lenient and moderate in his views, but it was in fact the prospect of war that finally reduced the witchcraft mania. A Swedish army was approaching with a view to invading Würzburg and the authorities had to concentrate on military matters rather than on witchcraft.

Famous English Witchcraft Trials

Chelmsford Witchcraft Trials

The Essex town of Chelmsford was much associated with witchcraft, and it was the scene of several witchcraft trials. The best known of the mass trials that took place there was the most shocking. The trials took place in 1645 and the notorious English witch-finder, Matthew Hopkins, was much involved.

The trials began with the interrogation of Elizabeth

Clarke, who was an old woman with one leg and a natural candidate for being accused of witchcraft, her mother having been hanged as a convicted witch. Elizabeth Clarke confessed to witchcraft and implicated several others, who in turn implicated others, and so on, until thirty-eight people were summoned to appear before the county courts on 29 July 1645. This kind of chain reaction of accusations was tragically common in witchcraft trials.

The Chelmsford trials are notorious partly for the scale and nature of the methods that were used to extract confessions. The use of physical torture inflicted by instruments was banned in England and so the accused were not subjected to such cruel devices as thumbscrews, the rack, strappado, etc. They were, however, mercilessly subjected to forms of what was known as induced torture. They were deprived of sleep, made to sit cross-legged on a stool for hours on end, and made to walk up and down continuously until they collapsed from exhaustion. Such methods were repeated until a confession was made, and they were employed largely at the instigation of Matthew Hopkins.

The trials are also infamous for the number of deaths. Of the thirty-eight people who were sent for trial only two were acquitted. Some of the others were imprisoned and some reprieved but seventeen of the women were executed by hanging.

For further details *see* Chapter 3, Chelmsford Witches, page 111.

Pendle Witchcraft Trials

One of the most notorious of the English mass witchcraft trials involved people from the Pendle Forest area of Lancashire, the trials taking place in Lancaster in 1612. At that time it was the largest witchcraft trial ever to have taken place in England. The trial was remarkable not only because of the numbers involved but because many of the accused were members of the same two feuding families.

Many of the charges were typical of those found in other English witchcraft trials. Several of them related to the killing of people by witchcraft, others to the harming of animals and others. An unusual slant was added to the trials by the fact that, shortly after the arrests, a rumour began to be circulated to the effect that members of the two families had got together in order to hatch a plot to blow up Lancaster Castle with a view to releasing their relatives imprisoned there.

Another remarkable feature of the trial was that one of the accused, Elizabeth Devine, was convicted largely on the evidence of her own children. These were a son in his twenties, who was of very limited intelligence, and a daughter aged nine, who was legally too young to give evidence, although such ineligibility on the grounds of age was often overlooked by the courts.

Both Elizabeth Devine's son and daughter testified to the fact that their mother had caused deaths by means of witchcraft and that she was known to have familiars, that is, supposed supernatural spirit companions in the form of animals. It was extremely easy in those days to find oneself in a situation in which one could be accused of either of these crimes. In the case of the second, all one had to do was a possess a cat or dog, have a cat or dog pass one's house or be so unfortunate as to have a hare appear in a field near one's house or a toad appear in one's garden.

At the end of the trials, ten of the accused were sentenced

to death in Lancaster by hanging on 20 August 1612, despite the fact that most of them were still protesting that they were innocent. One, Elizabeth Sowthern, had died in prison and another, Jennet Preston, had been hanged in her home town of York.

For further details *see* Chapter 3, Pendle Witches, page 166.

Warboys Witchcraft Trial

The main reason for the fame of this trial was the high social standing of those involved. The trial of Alice Samuel and her husband, John, and daughter, Agnes Samuel, took place at Huntingdon. They were charged with bewitching the five daughters of Robert Throckmorton, a wealthy squire from Warboys in Huntingdonshire.

The case had several of the elements that were later to characterise the notorious Salem Witchcraft Trials in the American colonies. At the heart of both trials was a group of girls who were suffering from strange fits and who blamed the accused for having caused these by means of witchcraft. In neither case could any medical diagnosis be made to account for their condition.

As in the case with Salem but on a lesser scale, hysteria developed, and other people began to claim to have been bewitched by the trio. Fear of witches was widespread. Other charges of causing death and harm to people and livestock, charges that were to be common in future witchcraft trials, were added to the original accusations.

The most serious of these charges concerned the death of Lady Cromwell, wife of the Throckmorton's landlord, Sir Henry Cromwell, and grandmother of Oliver Cromwell. She had tried to remove the influence that Alice Samuel was said to have over the girls and, although the attempt failed, she had offended Alice. Later Lady Cromwell complained of having nightmares in which she was attacked by Alice Samuel and her cat. She died about fifteen months later, and the Throckmortons laid her death at the door of the Samuels and their witchcraft.

Alice Samuel eventually confessed to being involved in witchcraft and to having consorted with the devil. She and her husband and daughter were all found guilty and hanged, their property being confiscated. Sir Henry Cromwell used this to fund an annual sermon against witchcraft to be preached in Huntingdon and this custom lasted until 1814.

Famous Scottish Witchcraft Trials

Aberdeen Witchcraft Trials

These trials, which took place in the Scottish city of Aberdeen, were noted for their sheer scale and the hysteria behind the witch-hunts that resulted in the trials. Pressure was used on the accused to get them to confess to a series of crimes traditionally associated with witchcraft, such as causing death by witchcraft, harming people and livestock by witchcraft, raising storms, etc, and also to cavorting with the devil and demons and indulging in lewd behaviour with them.

The pressure that was put on the accused included the use of the swimming test, by which the accused were bound hand and foot and cast into a stretch of water. If he or she floated, the accused was deemed to be guilty since the devil was assumed to be giving assistance, and if he or she sank, the accused was deemed to be innocent, although often dead (*see* Tests, Confession and Torture, page 71).

By April 1597 twenty-three women and one man had been put to death. They were first strangled at the stake and then burnt to ashes. Some of those taken before the court and imprisoned were so afraid of the treatment that would be meted out to them and the execution that might well be awaiting them that they took their own lives in prison. Even then they were not safe from the vengeance of the authorities. Their bodies were dragged through the streets until they were torn to pieces. Those who ended up with a verdict of not proven were punished also, having their cheeks branded and being banished from the city.

North Berwick Witchcraft Trials

These trials, held 1590–92, concerned a group of people supposed to belong to a coven that met at North Berwick, a town down the east coast of Scotland from Edinburgh. The trials were notable for several reasons. Among these was the high social standing of some of the accused and the fact that the king, James VI of Scotland, later James I of England, was involved, although as a prosecutor not as a defendant.

James was involved in two ways. First, some of the accused, supposedly aided by the Earl of Bothwell, were alleged to have used witchcraft to make attempts on his life, which, of course, amounted to treason. Second, he took a personal interest in the trials and insisted on taking part as an interrogator. The king had developed an interest in, and an antipathy to, witchcraft, and his involvement did much to encourage the hysteria that surrounded the trials. *See also* entries for Gilly Duncan (page 125), John Fian (page 127), Effie MacLean (page 157), Barbara Napier (page 163).

The trials were also noted for the use of savage torture. Witchcraft trials in England were barred by law from the use of physical torture, but this was not the case in Scotland. In these particular trials, several means were used, including thrawing – the jerking of the head violently and suddenly by means of a rope; thumbscrews or pilliwinks, by which the thumbs were crushed; and the use of a witch's bridle, which was placed round the head and attached to a cell wall by a very short chain so that the accused was unable to lie down and so was deprived of sleep. The trials also saw the use of turcas, a pair of pincers used to pull out the fingernails.

Apart from the royal involvement and the use of torture, the trials were noted for the sensational nature of the details revealed in the confessions of some of the accused, especially the details of the orgies indulged in at sabbats and of the attempts to murder the king by witchcraft contained in the confession of Agnes Sampson. The details supplied by her confession and those of some of the others were considered by some as to be so preposterous as to be completely incredible. The king, however, became very angry at any suggestions that the accused should be acquitted because their supposed confessions were so extremely unlikely.

At the end of the trials, Margaret Thomson had died under torture, and three people, Agnes Sampson, John Fian and Effie Maclean, were all executed. The first two were strangled and then burnt at the stake but Effie Maclean, although of high social standing, being the daughter of Lord Cliftonhall, was refused the leniency of strangling and was burnt alive.

This was very possibly a result of her connections with the Earl of Bothwell, who was believed to be behind plots on the king's life.

Bothwell himself was imprisoned for a time in Edinburgh Castle, but he had many supporters in the city and he escaped the death penalty. Although he had seen himself as a potential heir to the throne, he finally realised that he had failed to remove James from the throne and left Scotland to go into exile.

For further details *see* Chapter 3, North Berwick Witches, page 163.

Pittenweem Witchcraft Trial

This trial centred on a group of accused witches from the small fishing town of Pittenweem in Fife, Scotland, in 1704. It was remarkable for the ill-treatment of the accused, although there were no official executions, and for the fact that one of the accused was killed by an unruly mob after escaping. It was also notable for the fact that the original accuser, Patrick Morton, an apprentice blacksmith, who charged the first of the accused, Beatrice Laing, with causing him to suffer from fits and other ailments was later exposed as a fraud, having been helped in his deception with Patrick Cowper, the local minister, who was wont to warn his congregation of the dangers of witchcraft.

The accused included Mrs Nicholas Lawson, Janet Cornfoot, Isobel Adam, and Thomas Brown, as well as Beatrice Laing. Laing was subjected to sleep deprivation by the method known as watching and waking, by which the accused was subject to constant surveillance so that he or she would not fall asleep and to abrupt waking if sleep did occur.

After being forced to confess by this means and thereafter having retracted her confession, she was cast into solitary confinement in a dark dungeon for around five months.

Thomas Brown was subjected to food deprivation and died in prison of starvation.

Cornfoot was also forced to confess under the influence of torture, and she also withdrew her confession. She was then cruelly imprisoned in a steeple but escaped. A more dreadful fate awaited her, however, although not at the hands of the authorities. While hiding out at the house of another suspected witch, she was seized by a mob of people who were furious that she had escaped punishment. They angrily took the law into their own hands and beat her and strung her up so that they could pelt her with stones. She was then placed under a heavy door, which was then covered with heavy stones until she was pressed to death. Finally a horse and cart were driven back and forth over her corpse in case there were any vestiges of life left in it. No legal action was taken against the mob for this barbaric treatment, probably because the authorities were in sympathy with their action.

See Chapter 3, Pittenweem Witches, page 170.

Famous American Witchcraft Trials

Salem Trials

By far the most famous of the New World witchcraft trials took place in Salem in Massachusetts between 1692 and 1693. At their centre was the extraordinary behaviour of a group of girls and young women. A group of them, between the ages of twelve and twenty, began having fits, making strange noises and contorting their bodies. The group included eleven-year-old Abigail Williams and her cousin, nine-year-old Elizabeth Parris, the first two girls to become affected by the strange fits, eighteen-year-old Elizabeth Booth, seventeen-year-old Elizabeth Hubbard, nineteen-year-old Mercy Lewis, eighteen-year-old Susan Sheldon, twenty-year-old Mary Warren, sixteen-year-old Mary Walcott, twenty-year-old Sarah Churchill and twelve-year-old Ann Putnam. Later the hysterical behaviour spread to others.

Cause of the Hysteria

There seemed no reason for the girls' strange behaviour. After consulting with some other ministers of the church, the local minister, Samuel Parris, father of one of the earliest of the girls to be affected and one of the youngest, decided to call in the local doctor, William Griggs, who was the employer of another of the affected girls, Elizabeth Hubbard. Griggs was unable to come up with any medical diagnosis for the condition of the girls and finally stated that it was his belief that they had been bewitched.

In order to cure the girls, it was believed that whoever had been responsible for casting spells on them had to be identified and punished. The girls were approached, questioned and asked to tell the authorities who was responsible for their bewitched state. The real cause of the girls' behaviour remains unknown, although various suggestions have been put forward, ranging from repressed sexuality to the repression of women, to local politics and feuds, to the presence of a cereal disease, known as ergot, in the flour (which could have given rise to a form of food poisoning, causing hallucinations), to simple mischievous deception and a desire for attention. A popular and plausible suggestion is that Elizabeth Parris and Abigail Williams had become interested in the occult from stories about voodoo told to them by Tituba Indian, a servant who had been brought with him by the Reverend Parris from Barbados. Whatever the real reason, the girls appear to have been happy to go along with the witchcraft theory and lost no time in pointing the finger of suspicion at several local women.

Salem was not unique in having young girls at the centre of accusations of witchcraft. There were cases in England of young girls going into fits, sometimes later assumed to be epileptic fits, and then blaming their condition on some woman in the area, usually someone who had offended the accuser or her family in some way. In Salem it was the scale of the accusations, both in terms of the numbers of accusers and accused, that was remarkable. As to the acceptance of children's statements in witchcraft trials, this was not unique either. Although it was frequently disallowed by law, the presence of such a law was frequently deliberately overlooked.

The girls and young women who were the accusers lived in a small, relatively closed community and all knew each other well. They would have been used to telling each other stories and exchanging secrets. Conditions were therefore ripe for their affecting each other with their hysteria, especially if they had been dabbling in the occult. Once they began with their accusations, the whole thing took on a life of its own, and it would have been difficult for them to put a stop to it, even if they had wanted to. The speed with which the witchcraft hysteria spread was terrifying, and several factors contributed to this – feelings of political unrest, hostile raids by the Native

American Indians, a harsh winter that had resulted in poor crops and a smallpox epidemic. Salem was ready for a scapegoat and found it in witchcraft.

First Suspects

The girls were clever in their first choice of suspects. The first three to be named were not people whom the community would rush to defend since they were all in their own way on the very fringe of society and none was a member of the church. Tituba Indian, not surprisingly was the first to be named. She and her husband had been brought from their native Barbados by the Reverend Parris to be his servants, and she was already popularly supposed to have powers connected with the occult and had probably told her young charges, Elizabeth Parris and Abigail Williams, tales of voodoo and witchcraft from her native country. Next to be named by the girls were Sarah Good and Sarah Osborne. The former was a beggar woman and the latter an elderly cripple who had shocked the local community by allowing one of her servants to live in her house before marrying him.

Spectral Influences

These three outcasts of society were arrested and appeared at a preliminary before local magistrates John Hawthorne and Jonathan Corwin. The women were questioned and their accusers were allowed to be present at these interrogations. It was then that the occurrences began that were to make the Salem trials so remarkable. The girls were actually standing in front of the accused and patently obviously not being touched by them, yet they claimed that they were being pinched and bitten by them. It was the girls' contention that the women's spectres were harming them, although such spectres were visible only to the girls. They put on a convincing performance of being physically tormented and often pointed to some creature in the room, such as a bird in the rafters, as being the embodiment of the spectre of one of the accused.

Tituba's Confession

At the hearing Sarah Good and Sarah Osborne both denied any connection with witchcraft but, unfortunately for them, Tituba decided to make a confession associating herself with witchcraft. Worse, she identified Good and Osborne as fellow witches with whom she had attended meetings. Then she went on to claim that there was a coven of witches in Massachusetts led by a tall man dressed in black who had made her sign a book in blood. This was taken as evidence that Tituba had fulfilled one major condition for being a proven witch – she had signed a pact with the devil.

Tituba was the least likely of the accused to be acquitted on a charge of witchcraft. Even before the girls' behaviour and naming of names there had been rumours in the village about her connection with the occult. It is likely that she confessed to witchcraft thinking that by doing so she would save her life, it being the case in the American colonies, although not in mainland Europe, that making a confession would save one from execution.

The confession of Tituba and her talk of a coven struck fear into the hearts of local people. This was in part because of rumours that had circulated some years previously to the effect that Salem Village would be destroyed by a group of witches and that the household of the local minister would in some way be connected to this. As if in response to Tituba's confession and the increasing unease, the girls extended their range of accused. They appear to have been aided and abetted in this by Mrs Thomas Putnam, the mother of Ann Putnam, one of the accusers.

Accusations against the Godly

By this point the magistrates were much more inclined to believe the girls than they had been originally. In fact they were among those who encouraged the girls to name other names and did not question the veracity of their accusations, even when well-respected women in the village were accused. Among these were Martha Corey and Rebecca Nurse.

Martha Corey was acknowledged to be of excellent character, a devout Christian and regular churchgoer and wife of a local landowner. Nurse was one of the most respected people in the community and a regular churchgoer. Had such people been among the first of those accused by the girls, the magistrates and others would have been much more likely to look with incredulity on the claims of the girls. However, by this stage in the proceedings, there was no such thing as incredulity. The court simply accepted anything that the girls said, and they began accusing people from outside Salem Village itself, twenty-two communities being eventually involved. By this time several other adults had joined Mrs Putnam in claiming that they were being attacked by spectres of witches. Among these was John Indian, husband of Tituba.

There was often an element of vengeance in accusations of witchcraft. Such an element was very probably inherent in the charging of John and Elizabeth Proctor. They, too, were upstanding members of the community, but John Proctor had greatly offended one of the group of girls, Mary Warren. She was a servant in the Proctors' household and had been beaten by her master when she first started suffering from fits and accusing people of being witches. Following the beating, her fits and strange behaviour mysteriously disappeared. The other girls would not have looked on this kindly, and, indeed, they named Mary Warren as a witch also, which action acted as a warning to the other accusers not to change sides. As for Mary, she simply confirmed the girls' accusations and became one of them again.

Yet another unlikely person was accused by the girls. This was George Burroughs, a minister who had officiated at the church in Salem from 1680 until 1682. He had once lodged with the Putnam family and had incurred their hostility. He was accused by the girls of having his spectre bite and pinch them, and it was alleged that it was substantiation of this claim that the bite marks matched his teeth. Another serious accusation made by the girls was that he had made some of them sign a book supplied by the devil, thereby making them sign a pact with the devil. He was also accused of bringing them effigies, or poppets, representing people so that the girls could stick pins in them and therefore bring harm to the people concerned. More serious accusations, including murder and performing blasphemous rites mimicking Puritan services, were made against him. In fact, the conclusion was reached that he was the head of the coven described by Tibuta.

Doubts

And so the hysteria continued, and more and more people

were implicated. When a Justice of the Peace, Dudley Bradstreet, began to be concerned at the scale of the accusations and at the calibre of the people against whom they were levelled, he refused to sign any more arrest warrants. It was a sign of the times that he himself was promptly accused of witchcraft, but he was fortunate enough to escape before he could be tried.

In a similar category was John Willard. A local farmer, he was a deputy constable who had been involved in the arrest of the first suspects. However, as time went on and the whole thing appeared to be getting out of hand, he had second thoughts and was heard to say that the real guilty ones were the girls who had originally made the accusations. This was talk that was not to be tolerated and, having had wind of impending accusations against him, he fled. He was, however, not so lucky as Bradsheet and was captured, charged and hanged.

Second Thoughts and Retraction

As the hysteria continued, some of the girls appear to have had second thoughts and to have shown signs of admitting deception. Sarah Churchill actually admitted at one point to deceiving the court when her employer, George Jacobs, was arrested and interrogated. Mary Warren also began to indicate that deception had been involved when her employers, the Proctors, were thrown in prison, having had their property seized, leaving her in charge of their five children. Under threats from their co-accusers, however, both girls changed their minds and retracted their statements of deception.

Torture and Giles Corey

The Salem witchcraft trials, in common with others in the

American colonies and in England, did not involve the horrendous physical torture by instruments that were such a feature of the trials conducted in mainland Europe. There was, however, at least one exception to this absence of torture, and this was the torture of a Massachusetts landowner, Giles Corey.

The reason for his harsh physical torture was that he refused to plead and remained silent during the reading of the indictment against him. He thought that if he did not answer to the charge he could not be tried and convicted. It is possible that he was conscious of the fact that if he were to be convicted his property would be confiscated and thought that if he could avoid trial and conviction his property would remain his.

The authorities took a very dim view of his refusal to cooperate and decided to punish him into answering the accusation. The punishment was cruel and severe, especially in view of the fact that he was an old man of eighty. Corey was taken to a field, where he was held to the ground, naked, by a series of stakes. He was then covered by a large wooden plank on which were gradually placed more and more heavy stones. Corey still refused to cooperate and he was crushed to death. At one point the weights were so heavy that his tongue was pushed out of his mouth but Sheriff George Corwin simply pushed it back in with his cane.

Such cruel treatment was actually against the law in the American colonies, and because of this and because of the fact that there was still a degree of humanity in some members of the community, there was some concern expressed about what had happened to Corey. However, people were generally afraid to speak out and, in any case, the Putnam family brought new evidence against Corey and nothing was done.

Corey's treatment was thankfully unusual but, although those accused of witchcraft in Salem were not subjected to actual physical torture, their plight was nevertheless desperate. They were left to languish in prison, usually chained up, for months on end, not knowing what their fate was to be but fearing the worst, worrying about their families outside and all the while witnessing yet more people joining their ranks.

Politics and Trials

The length of time the accused were imprisoned before trial was in part a result of politics. In 1629, when Massachusetts Bay was established as a Puritan colony, it enjoyed the advantages of self-rule. However, in 1684 its independence was greatly restricted by the revocation of its original charter by the English courts. On the overthrow of its governor in 1688, when William and Mary ascended the British throne, the colony lost the authority that it needed to try capital cases. No trials of this nature could be held unless Massachusetts obtained a new charter conferring on it its former powers. Thus all the accused had to endure the misery of prison without a formal trial for a long time.

Finally, in May 1692, a new governor of Massachusetts was appointed by the Crown. His name was Sir William Phips, and he arrived having in his possession a new charter conferring the requisite authority to try capital cases. Thus the witchcraft trials of Salem could begin.

The Trials Begin

The new governor established what was known as a Court of

Oyer and Terminer, literally a court formed 'to hear and determine'. There had been much delay up until then but from 2 June, when the court first sat, little time was lost in trying and sentencing the accused witches. Indeed, the first of the accused, Bridget Bishop, was hanged on 10 June.

Spectral Evidence

As has been described above, the accusers claimed that the spectres of the accused appeared to them, sometimes in changed shape, and harmed them by biting and pinching them. Other people could not see these spectres unless the girls decided that a passing bird or animal was actually the spectre of one of the accused, but much credence was given to this spectral evidence

There were people who were worried about the use of such evidence. It was extremely unusual, and concern was raised about it from a theological as well as a legal point of view. The local ministers considered the matter and advised the courts against placing too much value on spectral evidence alone. This advice was by no means always taken by the court, many of whose members felt that their ability to harm the girls in spectral form was simply an extension of the pact that witches were traditionally supposed to make with the devil. In any case, the other forms of supposed evidence advocated by the ministers were neither factual nor reliable. Everything depended on the behaviour and claims of the accusers.

Falling at the Sight

One example of evidence of guilt concerned the behaviour of the accusers in the presence of the accused. If one of the accused looked at one of the accusers and the accuser collapsed, usually writhing in a fit, this was taken as clear evidence that the accused was a witch. No thought seems to have been given to the fact that this was simply an extension of the girls' hysteria and could easily be faked.

The Touch Test

Another supposedly reliable test involved the accusers being touched by the accused. If the accusers, who were still regularly afflicted by fits and attacks of gibbering, were touched by one of the accused in the course of a fit and immediately fell still and quiet then the accused was held to be a witch. Again this supposed evidence left the accused entirely at the mercy of the accusers.

Unjust Trials

Like many witchcraft trials elsewhere, the Salem trials could hardly be called just. Apart from the treatment meted out to Giles Corey (*see* page 48), there was an absence of physical torture. However, the accused were often convicted purely on unlikely evidence supplied by the accusers. Efforts were supposed to be made to obtain corroborative evidence, but such evidence was usually suspect. For example, if someone died in pain not long after having an argument with one of the accused, this could be taken as a clear indication that the accused had used witchcraft to bring death to his or her enemy as an act of vengeance. Anyone accused by the girls was thrown in prison to await trial, and after that conviction was almost a certainty.

For the most part the accused were denied the right to be represented by a lawyer. During interrogation, questions were expressed in such a way that made it almost impossible for the accused not to incriminate himself or herself. People were urged to confess on the grounds that such confessions would earn them a reprieve or at least save them from execution.

A case that illustrates the lack of justice involves Rebecca Nurse. This much respected member of the community was accused and tried but acquitted. On hearing the verdict, the girls, who were, as always, present at the trial, went into fits. The judge, Chief Justice Stoughton, was impressed with the reaction of the girls and immediately asked the jury to reconsider their verdict. Doubtless worried for their own safety, the members of the jury obliged the judge by reconsidering their decision and bringing in a verdict of guilty. Rebecca Nurse had many loyal friends, and they took a petition on her behalf to the governor to seek a reprieve. Initially this was granted, but later it was rescinded and Nurse was executed on 19 July 1692, along with Sarah Good, Sarah Martin and others.

Salem Confessions

The confessions were mostly acquired by means of question and answer sessions, which were standard elsewhere in witchcraft trials. Thus the Salem questions bore a resemblance to confessions obtained in the course of witchcraft trials in other parts of the world. Standard elements included consorting with the devil, signing a pact with him and flying to coven meetings on a broomstick.

Salem Executions

Those condemned to death on having been found guilty of witchcraft were executed by hanging. Their bodies were then placed in a shallow grave on Gallows' Hill, it being the accepted opinion that witches were consorts of the devil and so were not suitable candidates for Christian burial.

As has been mentioned above, Bridget Bishop was the first to be hanged, on 10 June. She was followed by Rebecca Nurse, Sarah Good, Sarah Martin, Elizabeth How and Sarah Wilds on 19 July. Further hangings followed on 19 August when John Willard, John Proctor, Reverend George Burroughs, Martha Carrier and George Jacobs met their deaths.

Burroughs caused much consternation when, just before his execution, he faultlessly recited the Lord's Prayer to the assembled crowd. It was a traditional sign of witchcraft for the accused not to be able to carry out such a feat. There were immediate demands for the minister's release. These were not satisfied by the girls' claims that the devil had helped him, because there was an accepted belief that reciting the Lord's Prayer was a deed beyond the capability of the devil. However, the Reverend Cotton Mather succeeded in convincing the crowd that the work of the devil was afoot, and Burroughs was hanged.

There were further executions on 22 September. Those who were hanged then included Martha Corey, Alice Parker, Mary Parker, Mary Esty, Margaret Scott, Ann Pudeater, Samuel Wardell and Wilmott Redd. Samuel Wardell had been so intimidated by the whole trial process that he had confessed to having signed a pact with the devil. To no avail did he retract his confession, and he was sent to the gallows. During the execution process he choked on smoke from the executioner's pipe, an act that was claimed by the girls to be prompted by the devil to prevent him from confessing.

In all nineteen people were executed. Even more were sentenced to death but for various reasons did not actually go to the gallows. These included Elizabeth Faulkner and Abigail Faulkner, who were reprieved on the grounds of pregnancy, and Ann Foster and Sarah Osborne, who died in prison.

The Beginning of the End

By the time of the above executions, the girls and others who had joined the ranks of the accusers were in a position of extreme power, but the scale of the accusations was beginning to worry a great many people. The girls, however, were unperturbed and quite clearly felt that they could accuse anyone and get away with it. In this assumption they were quite wrong. Their credibility was called into serious question when they had the temerity to accuse the wife of the governor, Sir Williams Phips.

This was a step too far, and on 29 October the governor dissolved the court that had been trying the supposed witches. There remained the problem of what to do about the many accused witches who were languishing in jail awaiting trial. A new court was established and deprived of the right to admit spectral evidence.

The debarring of spectral evidence was an extremely important measure. Without it most of the accused were acquitted by the various juries. A major problem with the new court from the point of view of the accused was that it still had William Stoughton as chief justice, and he had been zealous in making convictions. To some extent his influence was negated, but three people were convicted and he rapidly signed the warrants for their execution so that there would be no time for them to be reprieved. He also signed warrants for the execution of five people who had been convicted in September of the previous year.

Stoughton had hoped to have these executions carried out before anyone could prevent them. However, the governor was anxious to avoid more bloodshed and reprieved all the condemned people. The court sat for the last time on 9 May. All those accused were acquitted, and the Salem witchcraft hysteria was finally at an end.

Atonement

When the trials ended, many people began to question whether they should ever have taken place. In the absence of hysteria, what had gone on was viewed in the cold light of day. In 1696 many of the jurors made a public confession admitting that they had been guilty of error. They confessed that there had in fact been insufficient information relating to the cases and insufficient understanding on their part as to what was going on. They also begged forgiveness of the relatives of those who had been put to death.

Steps of atonement were taken by the clergy and state. A day of fasting and public apology, known as the Official Day of Humiliation, was held in 1697. In 1703 the colonial legislature of Massachusetts began to issue retroactive amnesties to the convicted and the executed and began in 1711 to grant a degree of financial compensation to the victims and their families.

As for the girls who were at the centre of the accusations and convictions, they were lucky enough to escape punishment. In general they appear not to have shown any desire to repent or ask forgiveness. Only the younger Ann Putnam seems to have been moved to make any form of reparation. It took her a long time to get around to this, fourteen years in fact, and the confession when it came was a little less than wholehearted. Delivering it in Salem Church, she laid much of the blame for 'the guilt of innocent blood' on Satan, claiming that he had deluded her.

The Aftermath

Salem never did shake off its notorious connection with witchcraft. More than three hundred years later the hysteria is still remembered and speculated over. The trials were terrible but Salem and the town of Danvers have benefited from them in that each year many tourists visit the area.

See also Chapter 3, Salem Witches, page 174.

Witch-finders

The witch-finder was an essential part of the witch trial. Sometimes witch-finders were officials appointed by the court involved in setting up witch trials, but often they were independent entrepreneurs who made a business out of the identification of witches. Motivated by a desire to make money out of their calling, and often by an inherent zeal to root out witchcraft by any means, they made it their business to acquaint themselves with the lore of witchcraft so that they could best catch their prey.

It was the witch-finders who gave the investigators the information that they needed to set the wheels of their investigations in motion. They tended not to be involved in the actual trials but spent a great deal of time snooping around villages and towns in which there was the slightest suggestion of witchcraft, listening to local gossip. Witch-finders were an itinerant breed, travelling from area to area as occasion called, and as soon as witchcraft was suspected the local authorities would call them in.

It was very much in the interests of the witch-finders to find evidence of witchcraft. Witch-finding was a well-paid profession, and it was common for them to be paid according to their success rate. Thus they were very unlikely to leave a place before having failed identified several witches and to having obtained confessions using such investigative methods as swimming (*see* page 77). Having identified as many as possible supposed witches in the area and seen them safely committed for trial, most witch-finders left the area and moved on to pastures new to find other rich pickings. The actual trials were not their concern.

However, they were inclined to direct their zeal at people of relatively low social standing or at people already known to be at odds with the authorities. They did not wish to antagonise local communities or local authorities by accusing popular or distinguished local residents. On the other hand, they were very much aware of the fact that the wealthier an accused witch was, the more money would come into the coffers of the courts and investigators and thus the more money they themselves would be likely to receive. (DE LANCRE, Pierre *see* Witchcraft Trial Judges, page 63.)

Matthew Hopkins

Witch-finders were particularly active in the German states in the early part of the seventeenth century, but they also operated elsewhere. Of the English witch-finders the most notorious was Matthew Hopkins, who gave himself the title of Witch-finder General and operated in the middle part of the seventeenth century in East Anglia and neighbouring areas. He is credited with having been the instigator of the conviction or execution of at least 230 accused witches, this figure representing more than all the other witch-finders together achieved during the years of witchcraft hysteria in England.

Hopkins studied law and was making a modest living as a lawyer in Ipswich when he had the idea of becoming a witch-finder. He moved to Manningtree in Essex, the latter having a tradition of being associated with witchcraft. At that point in the mid-1640s he knew little about witchcraft, although he had read *Daemonologie*, written by James I. However, he advertised his services to anyone who wished to root out witchcraft in his or her town or village.

He had chosen a good time at which to capitalise on witchcraft. It being in the middle of the Civil War (1642–48), the country was in the grip of political unrest and was looking for a scapegoat for its many ills. Witchcraft was as good a candidate as any. In addition, Puritan society already had a fear and hatred of witchcraft.

Hopkins' modus operandi was to collect local gossip and listen to tales of local feuds. The gossip and tales he would then try to turn into formal accusations of witchcraft and inform the authorities. His first victim was Elizabeth Clarke, an old crone from Manningtree with only one leg – (*see* Chapter 3, Chelmsford Witches, page 111). She was old and strange, and that made her an obvious candidate for being accused of witchcraft. Hopkins soon tortured her into confessing to consorting with the devil and to having familiars and also into naming others.

They in turn named others, and soon thirty-eight people had been charged, with many local people coming forward to give supposed evidence at Hopkins' instigation. By this time Hopkins had acquired an assistant, John Stearne, and now he took on four more, one of whom was Mary Phillips, and set to extend his witch-finding empire throughout other parts of England, such as Suffolk, Cambridgeshire, Huntingdonshire, Norfolk, etc.

By this time he was making an extremely good living since he charged extremely high fees, arguing that witch-finding was a very skilled task and that he was very successful. No elderly woman of strange looks or behaviour was safe from him, and his success at getting charges brought was phenomenal. His success was in great part due to his cruel methods, and he was greatly feared.

He was excessively zealous in many of the tortures, which stopped short of the use of torturing devices, banned in English courts. The tortures, applied in order to obtain confessions, included many of those mentioned above as induced torture – looking for the devil's mark and much given to the painful use of pricking to identify insensitive areas. His victims were also deprived of food and sleep, sleep deprivation being achieved by watching and waking. They were also made to walk up and down constantly until they fell down with exhaustion.

Hopkins showed both zeal and cunning when interrogating people with a view to getting them to confess to witchcraft. He and his assistants were adept at phrasing questions and in interpreting the answers in such a way that it was almost impossible for them not to incriminate themselves. The crimes of which he accused his victims were largely the traditional ones associated with witchcraft – death or injury of people or livestock by witchcraft, the keeping of familiars, the use of a broomstick to fly to coven meetings or sabbats, etc – and Hopkins was particularly fond of the crime that involved the accused signing a pact with the devil.

Hopkins' zeal was particularly successful in the town of Bury St Edmunds. There he was responsible for the accusation of nearly two hundred people. Nearly seventy of them are thought to have been executed. Among these was an old man, named John Lowes, who had been a Royalist and a member of the clergy. He was subjected to sleep deprivation until he confessed, one of the charges brought against him being that he had used witchcraft to sink a ship, although no motive was established.

The witch-finder went on to be responsible for other deaths in other counties, but his career, although terrible, was short. He began to come in for quite a lot of criticism. First his use of swimming was condemned and he was forced to stop using this method of obtaining confessions. He continued with his other methods, such as sleep deprivation and starvation, but soon he was publicly criticised for his excessive zeal in applying these and for his excessive fees.

In April 1646 the Reverend John Gaule, minister at Great Staughton in Huntingdonshire, objected to the presence of Hopkins and his assistants and publicly spoke against their investigations, saying that no wrinkled old woman was safe from them, however innocent. Hopkins ceased his witch-finding activities after that but wrote a pamphlet entitled *The Discovery of Witches* in defence of himself and his methods in 1647.

After that he is surrounded by mystery. Various possibilities have been put forward as to what happened to him but it is all a matter of speculation. Possibly the most likely explanation is that supplied by his assistant, John Stearne. He gave it as his opinion in 1648 that Hopkins had never enjoyed good health and had died of consumption in Manningtree in 1647.

Hopkins was such an important and hated figure that his seeming disappearance gave rise to various legends. One of these was quite possibly simply the result of wishful thinking on the part of those with cause to hate him. This legend has it that he was himself accused of witchcraft and subjected to the swimming test. He floated, thereby indicating his guilt, and was chased out of town, although one version of the legend has it that he was hanged.

According to another legend, he found England so hostile to him that he decided to follow some of his fellow Puritans and go to New England. Indeed, there has even been some unlikely speculation that as an old man he was involved in the Salem Witchcraft Trials.

There has also been speculation about what Hopkins' motives were. Certainly he charged a great deal of money, but greed alone was not thought to have motivated him. He appears to have genuinely believed in witchcraft and to have been filled with a religious-like zeal to stamp it out. On the other hand, he also appears to have enjoyed the power that his post of witch-finder gave him and the fear that people felt for him.

Witchcraft Trial Judges

Many of these were particularly cruel and many of them were simply interested in finding as many people as possible guilty.

Few made the effort to establish by absolute proof the guilt of the accused and few showed clemency.

Pierre de Lancre

One of the most notorious of such judges, in fact arguably the most notorious, was Pierre de Lancre, who conducted his operations in the Basque region of France. He was a French lawyer who was ordered by the king, Henri IV, in 1609 to go to the locality of Labourd, which it was claimed was being plagued by witches. It was de Lancre's task to eradicate this supposed plague of witches, and he took his task very seriously indeed, often combining the roles of witch-finder and trial judge.

De Lancre was convinced that the Basques, with their strange language and customs and their remote location, were exactly the kind of people who would be affected by witchcraft. He was also already convinced both of the actuality and dangers of witchcraft and filled with a determination to eradicate it.

He saw witchcraft everywhere and secured convictions on the slightest of evidence. Sometimes this supposed evidence comprised only completely uncorroborated accusations by children as young as five years old. Indeed, his judgements relied heavily on the testimony of children and on the use of torture to extract confessions.

De Lancre was particularly interested in gathering evidence of nocturnal orgiastic sabbats at which the devil was supposedly worshipped amid much merriment, nudity and lewd behaviour. It has been suggested that he was in fact fascinated by the descriptions of these and by the women who were supposedly involved in them. Indeed, he is said to have had some of the condemned witches dance for him while he played the flute during court intervals. Nevertheless, he punished harshly those confessing to being involved in sabbats.

He was also particularly interested in the potions and poisons supposedly brewed by those accused of witchcraft and in the shape-changing traditionally associated with witchcraft. The devil appears to have been something of an obsession with de Lancre, and there are various stories about claims that he is said to have made with reference to being attacked by the devil and witches in his bedroom.

The judge was infamous for the speed with which he processed trials and executions and for the number of people involved in these. He is said to have had executed as many as six hundred people by the time he was recalled in 1610, and it is not surprising that terror reigned in the area while he was present.

It was bad enough that de Lancre was so zealous and unreasonable in his attitude towards witchcraft but his attitude affected others. He wrote the details of his investigations and trials in three books, one published in 1612, one in 1622, and one in 1627, and these acted as guides to other witchcraft trial judges. He died in Paris in 1631.

Witch-hunts

The determined efforts to identify and root out witchcraft were known as witch-hunts, and these were pursued with remarkable zeal, particularly by professional witch-finders. No one, however innocent, was safe when full-scale witch-hunts were in progress, and they did much to incite the hysteria that was such a feature of the witchcraft period in history.

Although the word 'witch-finder' remained restricted to describing those who set about seeking out and accusing witches, the word 'witch-hunt' took on a more general meaning than its literal one. It came to mean an orchestrated campaign to identify and get rid of anyone holding dissenting or unorthodox views, this supposedly being done in the public interest. Later the expression was used in an even more general way to mean simply an orchestrated campaign to get rid of someone from a post, etc.

Charges of Witchcraft

The reasons for people being charged with witchcraft were often extremely nebulous. Since it was extremely difficult to define the exact nature of witchcraft, so it was even more difficult to prove it. Fortunately for the courts, proof was not something that bothered them overly much and people were charged on the flimsiest of evidence. The basis of many of the charges was often simply vengeance, the result of a local feud or simply chance if a determined witch-finder was at work. In continental Europe the basis of a charge was not important since confession was of prime importance, but in England confessions were supposed to be backed up by supposed proof. Therefore there were many traditional bases for charges.

Appearance

Often people had a preconceived idea of what a witch looked like – female, elderly, unattractive, solitary and strange. Thus any old woman who lived alone and was ugly or misshapen and indulged in strange behaviour, such as talking to herself, was a prime target. This was particularly true in England and Scotland. In continental Europe it was by no means unusual for young women to be selected as targets for accusations of witchcraft, especially if they came from wealthy families.

The archetypal old woman of the English witchcraft tradition was very vulnerable when it came to undergoing persuasion to extract a confession. She might have been already in poor health, whether mentally or physically, at the time of torture and likely to agree to anything. There is certainly reason to believe that the level of detail in some of the confessions relating to sabbats suggests mental problems.

Familiars

An old woman living alone in a village would be very likely to keep a pet. Alas this fact could only add to the likelihood of her being charged with witchcraft. It was part of witchcraft lore, especially in England and Scotland and later in the American colonies, that witches kept familiars. These were demons or imps supposedly assigned to witches by the devil to assist them in their witchcraft. Their outward appearance, however, was such as to enable them to blend into the background.

They often took the form of domestic animals, especially cats, but also dogs, and thus any old woman alleviating her loneliness by keeping a pet stood in great danger of being accused of witchcraft. Owning several cats was most unwise. However, it was not necessary actually to own a cat or dog in order to be accused of having a familiar. One passing the door was good enough to warrant a charge of keeping a familiar.

Virtually any creature, especially if it was relatively small, could be suspected of being a familiar. The hare was a particular favourite, and it was unfortunate indeed if a hare made an appearance in a field near the home of someone already suspected of witchcraft. Another creature much associated with witchcraft was the toad, and it was as well not to have one pop up in one's garden. The crow and the blackbird were other favourites, but a creature such as a mouse, rat, ferret, hedgehog, or even a bee, grasshopper or ant could be suspect also, and there were more unusual ones. Since it was impossible never to come into contact with a small animal the charge of having a familiar was a common one.

Witches were popularly believed to take good care of their familiars, often baptising them, feeding them well and rewarding them with drops of their own blood. This blood was thought to be sucked by the animals from the fingers of the witches or from protuberances or spots on the skin. Some witches were even thought to have an extra nipple for this very purpose.

Familiars were traditionally held to be able to disappear at will and to have the capability of taking on more than one shape. Their function was to help their owners carry out their various acts of bewitchment. They were supposedly able to execute such deeds as turn milk sour and injure livestock. Sometimes they were alleged to substitute for broomsticks to enable witches to fly through the air to coven meetings.

Healing

It was common before the days of chemical medicines, and indeed becoming relatively common again now, for people to use things gathered from the countryside to try to heal or cure illness or wounds. There was often one person in a village who was particularly skilled in the making of herbal medicines and ointments. Sometimes he or she would have acquired particular skills in healing.

Such skills were useful to the community, but having a reputation for possessing them was very unwise during the period of witchcraft hysteria. Having the ability to heal in any way was seen as evidence of the supernatural. Anyone with a reputation for healing or for supplying medicinal herbs or potions was likely, indeed, to be accused of witchcraft.

Prophecies and Fortune-telling

Anyone who was credited with being able to foretell the future was at risk of being accused of dabbling in witchcraft. Divination was held to be supernatural and so probably a gift from the devil.

Causing Death, Injury or Damage by Witchcraft

It was common for someone to be accused of using witchcraft to kill someone. The accused killer did not have to be anywhere near the victim when death occurred. That was the beauty of witchcraft. At particular risk of such a charge was someone who had a particular reason for disliking someone who died or was killed.

Sometimes it was not death but injury or illness that occurred. For example, a person could be accused of witchcraft if someone started having fits, as was the case in the celebrated Salem Witchcraft Trials. It was not always people who were involved in accusations of death or injury by witchcraft. Often the basis of an accusation was that someone had killed or caused injury or illness in farm livestock. Hens that stopped laying or cows that ceased to yield any milk were enough for this charge to be made.

The failure of crops could also be conveniently blamed on alleged witches.

Storm-raising

The problem with many of the charges made against supposed witches was that, although they were impossible to prove, they were often difficult to disprove, and it was common to assume an alleged witch guilty until proved otherwise. If someone accused of witchcraft lived by the sea and a storm occurred that resulted in the wreck of or damage to a ship, he or she could readily be accused of storm-raising, a common traditional feat of witches. It was particularly dangerous for the accused if there was someone on board the ship who for some reason was disliked by him or her.

Storm-raising was a favourite charge in communities near the sea where seafaring was a regular part of life, but charges of storm-raising could also be brought against people who lived in inland communities. If storms destroyed crops, a suitable candidate for being accused of storm-raising was sought out.

Flying by Broomstick

The broomstick was traditionally held to be the preferred form of transport for witches. Questions relating to this were a standard part of the interrogation process carried out in order to elicit confessions. The standard confession would thus contain an admission of flying by broomstick. Occasionally neighbours would claim that they had seen the accused fly out of her window on a broomstick.

Devil's Pact

Admitting that he or she had entered into a pact with the devil, traditionally written in blood taken from the witch's left hand, was a standard part of an accused witch's confession, elicited by standard interrogation and usually by torture. The instigators of the Inquisition in continental Europe were particularly keen on pacts with the devil since these were a clear sign of heresy, and they were anxious to see witchcraft viewed as a form of, or as an extension of, heresy. The fact that so many people, under the influence of terrible torture, eventually confessed to signing pacts with the devil gave credence to the belief that such a thing actually existed and was an essential part of witchcraft.

There were two possible reasons for supposedly signing such a pact with the devil. One of these, and the one that was most common in the case of witchcraft, was that the devil, in return for the signing of the pact and so declaring allegiance to him, would help the witch in any way possible with the pursuit of his or her magic. The supplying of a familiar was often part of the deal, and the magic often was assumed to be a means of causing harm to others. The other reason to sign such a pact was the Faustian one where someone supposedly signed a pact with the devil giving the devil his or her soul in exchange for unbridled pleasure, wealth, power, etc.

The idea of signing a pact with the devil was of great importance in the witchcraft trials in mainland Europe where people could be convicted of witchcraft on the basis of confession alone. In England worries about witchcraft concentrated on the harm that witches could do rather than on the fact that they had turned their back on God. Thus the devil's pact as such did not play a major role in most English witchcraft trials, although the witch-finder Matthew Hopkins (*see* page 58) did obtain confessions of signed pacts and used these as evidence.

The pact could be either oral or written, but the latter was more popular as a reason for levelling an accusation of witchcraft. The signing ceremony might take place privately, sometimes under the auspices of another witch, or it might take place publicly at a sabbat. The courts much preferred the public ceremony because then they might acquire not only the confession of the person who did the signing but supposed proof from others who had attended the sabbat and allegedly witnessed the signing. Conveniently for the courts, it was apparently traditional for the devil to keep the signed pact and so it could not be produced as physical proof of an association with witchcraft.

Attendance at Sabbats

It also became a standard part of a witch's confession that he or she had attended a sabbat (*see* Chapter 4, page 286), a great celebratory gathering of witches, usually held in some remote location and characterised by feasting, drinking and dancing, often in the nude, uninhibited, indiscriminate sexual encounters and worship of the devil. Having a witch confess to having attended a sabbat was a good opportunity for the courts to illustrate just how lacking witches were in morality and piety.

Tests, Confession and Torture

At the height of the witch trials, the cruellest tortures imaginable were used on people accused of witchcraft in order to force a confession out of them and in order to make them give the names of their accomplices in the black art or to identify other people whom they suspected of witchcraft. It was deemed that justice demanded that a person accused of witchcraft should not be executed unless he or she confessed to the crime. Furthermore, by confessing, the supposed witches would be saving their mortal souls. Therefore all manner of means were used to make sure that people did confess, and this was far from being justice.

The tortures themselves must have been agonising beyond comprehension. Many of the devices of torture imposed such unbearable pain that people would agree to anything, including confessing to witchcraft, in order that the torture and pain would stop, although some of the accused retracted these confessions on cessation of the pain. Furthermore, many of the people accused of witchcraft were elderly and their bodies and minds were far from being able to withstand even the mildest of such tortures. The tortures themselves often resulted in serious injury, death or madness. Others of the accused were already mentally unstable and the tortures were almost guaranteed to send them insane.

The prevalence of torture varied from area to area. Although there was some torture inflicted on the accused in the Salem Witch Trials, this was on a far lesser scale than in Europe and in general torture was not much used in witch trials in America.

In England and Wales, where instruments of torture were not allowed according to the common law of the countries, the level and the nature of the torture was considerably less extreme than it was in such countries as Germany, although forms of it were more widely used than in America. Scotland, however, did not fare so well, and barbarous forms of torture were used there, particularly in the reign of King James VI, later James I of England.

It was in Germany, France, Switzerland and Italy that the worst tortures took place. The crime of witchcraft was deemed to be a crime against God, and the Inquisition had already established a frightening range of tortures against suspected heresy before attention was turned towards witchcraft. Witchcraft was added to the list of heresies in 1320, and Pope Innocent VIII issued a papal bull against witchcraft in 1484. Persecution of witches was then widespread and the ruthless inquisitorial system well in gear.

A major guide to the inquisition of witches was *Malleus Maleficarum,* compiled by the Dominican Inquisitors of Pope Innocent VIII, Heinrich Kramer and James Sprenger. They emphasised the need for confession and the need to employ torture in order to extract this. There were guidelines and set procedures laid down for the courts to follow.

Tests

There were a number of tests undertaken to identify supposed witches. They were not categorised as tortures but some of them caused much pain and distress. Tests used to establish an association with witchcraft included the following.

Shaving and Probing

The accused was first of all asked to confess. Sometimes even at this stage people were so aware of the kind of ordeal that lay in front of them that they simply gave in and confessed to witchcraft, although they had absolutely no connection with it. If such confession was not forthcoming then he or she was stripped naked and shaved. This procedure may not have been construed as torture but it certainly caused embarrassment and humiliation and, in the case of women, was not infrequently carried out by a member of the opposite sex. The accused were shaved partly in case a demon might have hidden in their body hair with a view to helping them in the course of a trial and partly because a charm with magical powers might have been similarly secreted. For these same reasons the accused had to submit to have having all their orifices probed.

The Devil's Mark

Then the accused were often subjected to a search for evidence of the devil's mark. It was the belief of those zealously intent on seeking out and exterminating witchcraft that the devil made a permanent mark on the bodies of those who had sworn allegiance to him, although there was a school of thought that he made such a mark only on those whom he considered to be unreliable. The search for such a mark was one of the major tests for the presence of witchcraft.

The devil was popularly held to mark the body of his initiates in a number of ways. These included licking, kissing or touching a particular spot, raking his claws across the body or branding it with a hot iron. Such marks were frequently thought to be difficult to locate and required the most rigorous and embarrassing of searches. They were thought to be often located under the armpits, under the eyelids, and in any of the body cavities. Such a mark was considered to be definite proof of being a witch, but if the investigator was a particular zealous one and bent the rules a bit then practically any mark on the body could be construed as being a devil's mark. This was bad news indeed since few of us have mark-free bodies.

Supposed experts on the subject claimed that a mark which could be categorised as a devil's mark was easily distinguishable from harmless body blemishes, but the categorisation system was not all that foolproof, even if such a thing as a devil's mark had actually existed. It was believed that the devil's mark was insensitive to pain or incapable of bleeding and that the best way to locate such a spot was to prick the accused person all over with a sharp pin or lance until such a spot, which might be a wart, cyst, mole, scar, callus or thickened area of skin, was identified. A particularly nasty trick consisted of cutting someone so painfully on one part of the body so that all attention was focused on that and any other pain in another part of the body went unnoticed.

All in all it was unusual for an accused person to escape having an insensitive area or an area that would not bleed identified on his or her body.

There was another less common form of devil's mark. This supposedly took the form of a shape or figure. This could be a cloven hoof, traditionally associated with the devil or a hare, often connected with witchcraft, or even something seemingly innocuous such as dormouse. Since with a bit of imagination such a mark on the body could be said to resemble just about anything, this was a very easy way in which to incriminate supposed witches (*see also* Chapter 4, page 254).

Pricking

If no mark could be found, and it was rare for a zealous investigator to admit defeat, then this was not always the end of the story. Conveniently for the investigators intent on discovering evidence of witchcraft, it was believed that the devil did not always leave a mark when claiming someone for his own. Apparently he sometimes just made a small area of the body of his devotee insensitive. Being searched for such an area could be extremely painful as pins were jabbed into the body all over and it was unlikely that the investigators employed gentle tactics. This was known as pricking.

The devil's mark test was a very common one in the identification of witches and the finding of anything that could possibly be construed as one was taken as proof positive of witchcraft. Evidence of such a mark and an accusation of witchcraft were often enough to convict, and many people were executed simply because they had blemishes on their bodies.

Margaret Murray (*see* page 13) put forward the theory that devil's marks did actually exist. She did not maintain that the devil had put them there but suggested that they might have been a form of tattoo with which people practising witchcraft marked themselves. This was part of her wider theory that witchcraft actually did flourish at the time of the witch trials and was part of an organised pagan religion with its roots in very early times, having been driven underground by the coming of Christianity. Her theory is now largely discredited by historians, although they were accepted by several of her contemporaries, but many modern people who describe themselves as witches still believe that witchcraft is an ongoing ancient religion with its own established rites.

Lord's Prayer

One of the tests for witchcraft consisted of getting the accused to recite the Lord's Prayer. This had to be repeated accurately and without stumbling. If any mistakes or pauses occurred, the accused was held to be unable to complete this holy task because of his or her association with the devil. Since most of the accused would likely be trembling with terror and incapable of thinking or speaking clearly, the number of people who failed to pass this test was very high.

Swimming

Technically, swimming was not an official test of an accused witch's guilt. In England, indeed, the swimming test was declared illegal by Henry III in 1219. However, it was often used as a kind of unofficial initial test when suspicions about a person's association with witchcraft first arose and was frequently conducted by a mob of villagers with absolutely no legal backing. Sometimes the courts regarded swimming as a valuable first step in a witch trial and turned a blind eye to the fact that it was illegal. Swimming, also known as ducking, was an ancient test of guilt that had its origins in Babylonia and was used in England pre-1219 for a range of suspected crimes before becoming associated with witchcraft.

This test of guilt consisted of binding the accused's hand and foot, often with the right thumb bound to the left big toe and vice versa, before throwing him or her into a stretch of water, such as a pond, lake or river. If the accused floated then it was taken as a sign of guilt, the theory being that the devil was helping his own to survive. If on the other hand, the accused sank, then it was supposed that the person was innocent. This, however, was often small comfort since many of the accused who sank drowned before they could be helped out of the water. Sometimes the plight of the accused was even worse because he or she was sewn into a sack before being thrown into the water.

The swimming test grew more popular in England after it

was commended by James VI of Scotland and I of England in his book *Daemonologie* (1597). James was convinced that there was witchcraft abroad in his kingdom and he was determined to root it out. Swimming, he felt, would help him to do this. He was convinced that the reason people who floated were considered to be guilty of practising witchcraft was that the water would not receive into it people who had been baptised in water as Christians and then renounced this sacrament when they began associating with the devil.

Confession

Having had supposed evidence of the devil's mark found on them, the accused was usually given the opportunity to confess. It was considered an essential part of the witchcraft investigation process that the accused admitted to being a witch, as opposed to being allegedly proved to be one. The Continental courts were reluctant to sentence a supposed witch to be executed unless a confession had been obtained, although they do not appear to have been unduly concerned about whether there was any actual proof that witchcraft was involved. In England the situation was rather different since the courts usually required some form of proof, however flimsy, to back up the confession.

Since the barbarity of the witch trials, especially in mainland Europe, gradually became well known there were those who felt that they might as well make a voluntary confession right away, thinking that if they were going to be tortured into confessing anyway they could save themselves a great deal of pain. Their logic, however, tended not to pay off.

The investigators were not disposed to look kindly on these instant confessions. They felt, rightly, that they had been made to avoid pain and might well be false. They frequently were false but not in the suspected way. It was a case of innocent people confessing to witchcraft to avoid torture, but the investigators assumed them to be guilty but to have given false details in their confessions. The only way to make sure that the correct details were given, they reasoned, was to torture these instant confessors into giving the 'real' details.

As an aid to the obtaining of a so-called voluntary confession, details of the kind of ordeal to which the accused would be subjected in order to secure an eventual confession were often relayed by the investigators, doubtless with glee.

The threat of torture, especially when it was graphically described, was quite enough to have some of the accused, although there appear to have been surprisingly few of these, agreeing to make a confession that was then deemed to be voluntary. If no voluntary confession was forthcoming then it was a case of proceeding to the next stage of the trial – the torture.

The use of the most remarkably brutal torture was common in Europe, although not so in England or the American colonies. Basically the policy of the European courts appears to have been that the accused be tortured until a confession was made. The physical agony was such that many died in the course of torture, a blessed relief for them, although it was the aim of the investigators to keep them alive. Others were driven to 'confess' to crimes that they had never committed just to have the pain stop. Many were probably driven mad.

Throughout the various tortures the accused was asked to confess. Various questions were put, and these often followed a formula, concentrating on such issues as meeting the devil, causing death by casting spells on the victim and the use of broomsticks as transport to sabbats. It is because the questions were formulaic that the confessions were so formulaic, thereby often closely resembling one another.

In order to be valid in court, the confession had to be documented. With this in mind a clerk recorded the proceedings when the inquisitor was putting his questions and demanding a confession. It was the fact of confession rather than the details that had to be recorded. There were so many accused and the questions so formulaic that the accused's confession was very rarely recorded in any detail.

Having confessed while being tortured, the accused then had to confirm the confession after a time of recovery from the torture. This was apparently to avoid any suggestion that the confession had been extracted by force – which of course it had.

It was not uncommon for confessions to be made just before the scheduled time for an execution. This was often done to lessen the pain of death. Most witches who had confessed fully to their association with witchcraft were accorded the supposed leniency of being strangled to death before they were burned at the stake. While hardly a pleasant death it was preferable to the slow agony of being burnt alive. Confession at the stake proved popular with the crowds who gathered at the place of execution as it added to the drama of the occasion.

One of the remarkable features of confessions to witchcraft is the extent to which many of them implicated other people. Perhaps this was because the confessor cherished a hope, which usually proved vain, that appearing to be helpful to the authorities would persuade them to show a degree of clemency. Perhaps there was an element of vengeance relating to past quarrels. Perhaps the naming of names was done in the spirit of wishing others to share the same misfortune as the confessor was experiencing. Or perhaps it was just part of the formulaic question and answer sessions which typified many of the witchcraft trials. At any rate, fear must have struck people's hearts if anyone they knew was charged with witchcraft.

Not confessing, even under the duress of the most severe torture, was certainly not regarded as evidence of innocence. Quite the reverse. Being able to withstand the level of physical pain to which the accused was subjected was held to be extremely unnatural and clear evidence that the devil was at work helping his initiate. In the end, if torture failed the only solution that offered itself to the investigators was execution.

Retraction

It was by no means unknown for people to try to withdraw their confessions after they had stopped being tortured and had had time to reflect on what had happened. This rarely did them any good. Usually the retraction of a confession simply resulted in renewed torture until they withdrew their retraction. Recanting was seen as evidence that the devil was using his wiles to encourage the accused to adopt delaying tactics and prevent the due process of the law. Just as some of those accused of witchcraft confessed just before execution, so did some of them chose that moment to withdraw their confessions. Again this usually resulted in more torture being administered.

Induced Torture

The degree of torture and the nature of it varied. In England physical torture using barbaric instruments of torture was not nearly as common as elsewhere. This was in part because the

Inquisition, which was behind much of the torture imposed on accused witches in mainland Europe, had never made much ground in England. Its lack of success was to a great extent owing to the tenets of the English law, which debarred the courts from accepting confessions unsupported by other proof and disallowed the forms of torture that were a major part of the Inquisition's investigations.

Instead, in England what was known as induced torture was used. This was an insidious form of torture not requiring much in the way of instruments but was nevertheless capable of causing much pain and distress. Such forms of torture included depriving the accused of food or water. Sometimes they were fed a diet of salty food and then deprived of water so that they suffered the distress of terrible thirst. In particular there were two extremely common forms of this type of torture – watching and waking, and walking.

Watching and Waking

This was an example of induced torture and was much used in England, especially by Matthew Hopkins, the notorious English witch-finder, the more extreme forms of torture practised in Germany and elsewhere being not allowed. Its aim was to deprive the accused of sleep until a confession was obtained.

Everything was done to prevent the accused from sleeping. Sometimes it was just a question of the guards roughly waking people who were clearly about to sleep, but some of the methods used were more cruel. For example, those whom the guards wanted to keep awake might be rendered unable to lie down or even to sit down to sleep because of being chained to the cell wall by means of an iron bridle attached to the head and a very short iron chain. Another cruel way of keeping people from sleeping was to make them sit cross-legged on a stool for hours on end.

Walking

This was another form of induced torture. It does not sound anything like as horrific as some of the methods of torture allowed on the continent but it had a terrible effect on those who were subjected to it and was frequently efficacious in obtaining confessions. As the name suggests, this particular torture involved the accused being forced to walk up and down all the time, sometimes for days at a time, without any rest until exhaustion and collapse set in.

Torture by Device

In mainland Europe the use of barbaric methods of torture using various devices was widespread. It is for that reason that courts there had such a reputation for obtaining convictions. In the light of the pain experienced by the accused it was virtually impossible to maintain and prove one's innocence. There were degrees of torture, and if the accused successfully tolerated one form then the investigators simply moved on to one further up the scale of agony and terror.

Ironically, the cost of administering the torture, including the travel and accommodation expenses of the torturer, and also of mounting the witch trial generally, was met by the accused. If a person on trial for witchcraft had enough money then his or her funds were seized or the estate confiscated after execution. On the other hand, if the accused was impoverished or did not have enough money to pay for the considerable expense of being tried and tortured for witchcraft, then the authorities simply made the accused's relatives responsible for meeting the bill.

Rack or Ladder

The rack was not used either in England or in Scotland, which had quite a reputation for savage torture, but was used throughout Europe, particularly in France. It was a device for stretching the victim to an agonising extent. The prisoner would be laid horizontally on the rack or ladder and have his or her limbs bound to it with ropes tied with a tourniquet knot. This knot could then be tightened by gradually twisting it, the ropes controlled by it stretching the accused's arms and legs and thus the whole body. The rack, which often broke bones and tore muscles, was a horrendous form of torture but by the standards of Inquisition-style torture it was by no means the worst and tended to be used in the relatively early forms of torture to give the accused a taste of what was to come.

Boots

Known also as Spanish boots, bootikins or cashielaws, the device called boots was also a stretching instrument. It consisted of lengths of wood bound together lengthways. These lengths of wood were fitted on the legs of the accused from the ankles to the knees and were either gradually tightened by hand or knocked together with a wooden mallet. The result was broken bones and torn flesh and muscles and often legs that never walked again.

Thumbscrews

This form of torture did for the thumbs what the boots did for the lower limbs. They consisted of vices on which the thumbs of suspected witches were crushed by gradual tightening of the vices unmercifully until blood spurted. A variation on this theme of torture was the application of such vices to the toes.

Spider

The spider was a sharp iron fork used in torture. Many of those accused of witchcraft were women and the spider was used to cause injury to their breasts.

Red-hot Irons and Pincers

Much had been learnt by the practitioners of the Inquisition about inflicting pain and they were certainly not unaware of the agony to be inflicted by the use of red-hot instruments. Red-hot pincers were used to tear flesh unmercifully and were even used to tear off women's breasts.

Red-hot irons were used to burn flesh and to gouge out eyes but were also used to insert into the vagina or rectum. There was also a red-hot iron test for witchcraft. Accused witches were told to grab hold of a red-hot iron. If they succeeded in holding it they were deemed to be guilty but, by this stage in the torture proceedings, they had been subjected to such pain that they had acquired a certain amount of insensitivity to pain.

Turcas

This device was used to tear out fingernails, the torture being made severe by driving needles into the quicks after the application of the turcas. Although England was largely free of the more extreme forms of torture, particularly those that employed devices of torture, because of restrictions imposed by the legal system, this was not so true of Scotland. As an example of this, Scotland allowed the use of turcas, the device being used in the trial of John Fian (*see* Chapter 3, page 127).

Thrawing

This form of torture, popular in Scotland, involved the head being bound with ropes. It was then jerked from side to side, causing much pain and damage to the neck. An exceptionally painful refinement of this had the ropes attached to a collar studded with spikes.

Strappado

This was a more extreme form of torture, extensively practised in mainland Europe. It involved tying the hands of the accused behind their backs prior to attaching them to pulleys. The accused were then hoisted to the ceiling, heavy weights sometimes being attached to the legs or feet to increase the pain and injury. The result of this form of torture was the dislocation of shoulders and other joints. In order to increase the agony imposed by this torture it was often combined with the use of thumbscrews.

Squassation

This refers to an extreme form of strappado used on those accused who had refused to succumb to other forms of torture. The victims of this were treated to the same initial process as for strappado, heavy weights being strapped to their lower limbs as a matter of course. Then the pulley ropes holding them were suddenly released and the accused fell to the floor, only to have the fall suddenly brought to a halt by the tightening of the ropes. People who were subjected to this form of torture were lucky to escape with any undislocated bones.

Water Torture or Ordeal

A particularly barbaric form of torture involved forcing the accused to swallow great quantities of water, sometimes boiling water to add to the pain, along with lengths of knotted cord or cloth. The cord or cloth was then yanked back up violently and suddenly, and this often had the effect of disembowelling the accused.

Other Forms of Torture

There were several other forms of torture, for there was really no limit to the lengths the investigators would go to in continental Europe to ensure a conviction. Hands and ears were cut off, burning feathers dipped in sulphur were applied to sensitive areas such as the armpits and groins, fingers were immersed in pots of boiling oil and bodies were immersed in boiling-hot baths treated with lime.

Post-confession Torture

Those of the accused who confessed did so because they were driven to this action by the agony of the ordeal of torture. They probably thought that such confessions would bring an end to their pain until they faced their executioners. Frequently this was not the case, especially in mainland Europe. Those skilled in the techniques of the Inquisition were not likely to let their victims go lightly. Thus it was quite common for those condemned to die for supposed witchcraft to be subjected to flogging or branding on their way to the place of execution. At this time also, fingers, hands and tongues were sometimes cut off and nailed to the gallows. Presumably this was meant to act as an extra grisly warning to others not to become involved in witchcraft.

The End of Torture

By the middle of the seventeenth century the full horror of the savage torture to which accused witches in Europe were subjected began to be appreciated by those in power. Several German rulers, notably the Duke of Brunswick, abolished the use of torture in the areas ruled over by them and also made efforts to get other rulers to follow suit.

Execution

The Inquisition had established burning at the stake as an appropriate punishment for heretics and the same punishment was frequently meted out to witches. Witches were regarded in much the same light as heretics since they were presumed to have turned their backs on God in favour of the devil. Fire was seen as a means of purification, and in addition it was thought that only by burning witches to ashes could all remnants of their powers be destroyed. Even children sometimes were punished in this way, although many of them were punished by imprisonment or flogging rather than execution.

Burning at the stake was a very painful death, particularly if the wood used was green and therefore slow to kindle and burn, resulting in a slow as well as agonising death. In Italy and Spain witches were often subjected to the agony of being burnt alive at the stake. In other countries, such as France, Germany and Scotland, they were either strangled at the stake or hanged before being burnt, but this clemency could be revoked if the accused retracted a confession of witchcraft at the time of execution. Courts in England and the American colonies usually ordered those found guilty of witchcraft to be hanged and they were burned alive only if found guilty of what was regarded as treason.

The execution of a witch was a major public occasion, and crowds would gather enthusiastically to view the spectacle, which was meant to serve as a warning to others as well as punishment to the person condemned. People facing execution were often expected to repeat their confession or otherwise confirm their guilt after having had read out a list of the crimes of which they had been found guilty. Sometimes they added to the excitement of the crowd by withdrawing their confession and thus deprived themselves of the privilege of being hanged or strangled before going to the stake.

Usually the execution took place shortly after the sentencing, indeed as soon as an executioner was summoned and the fire built. Local people were advised of the coming event by the tolling of church bells or by the blaring of trumpets. As was the case with the expenses for the trial and torture, the expenses of the execution were paid out of the condemned person's estate or by relatives.

In Scotland the execution was not so speedy. The days before the burning of a witch were often taken up by fasting and preaching. The condemned witch was usually first strangled and then burnt but not too much care was taken to check that death by strangling had actually occurred. It was not unknown for the condemned person simply to be unconscious or semiconscious when committed to the fire. If they were still alive and attempted to get out of the fire there were many willing helpers to push them back in again.

Summary

At the time when witchcraft mania was at its height it was all too easy to be accused of witchcraft. In England, if you were a poor, elderly, solitary, rather ugly woman and slightly strange, the outlook was bleak. If you had as a pet a cat or a dog and were interested in herbal medicine and natural healing then you were exceptionally at risk. In parts of Europe it was not poor, elderly women who were at risk but the affluent. The courts and state were very conscious of the fact that the estates of those accused of witchcraft would be forfeited if they were convicted and executed.

Even if you fulfilled neither of these criteria you were not safe. In fact hardly anyone was safe from accusations of witchcraft. When people were tortured into confessing, either by the horrific devices common in mainland Europe and in Scotland or by the more subtle means common in England, they mostly showed a tendency to name others. If you knew any of the accused, if you had offended any of them, or even if you were just known to them, you were at risk of being named as a witch. People who had been repeatedly tortured until they made a confession of something with which they probably had no association were in no mental state to be rational.

Once you had been charged, the outlook was indeed black. It was particularly bad if you were in one of the mainland European countries, particularly France or Germany, and Scotland was not very far behind them in this respect. All these countries allowed physical torture by horrific devices, and the mainland European countries allowed convictions and executions on the basis of confession only. Given the fact that people were tortured until they did confess, and the fact that if they somehow managed to withstand the torture and refused to confess they were executed since this was taken as a sign that the devil was helping them, the vast majority of those accused were convicted and most of them executed.

In England things were not quite so bad in that the horrific devices of torture were not allowed and in that the accused were not supposed to be convicted on the basis of confession alone. However, there was much turning of a blind eye to some of the practices that were undertaken when the hysteria was at its height. These included letting underage children testify. When the notorious English witch-finder, Matthew Hopkins, was at work it is said that he used extremely cruel means to obtain a confession, such as swimming, starvation and sleep deprivation, and that he recommended that people be charged on the flimsiest of supposed proof, such as the fact that they kept cats as pets. Also it appears that he was not above recommending conviction by confession only.

All the advantage was on the side of the accusers when it came to the trial. Often the accused were debarred from being legally represented and often they were not told the actual substance of the accusations against them nor the identity of their accusers. People were reluctant to offer to speak on behalf of the accused because they were likely to be assumed to be his or her associates and themselves accused of witchcraft. Those who were brave enough to volunteer to give evidence for the defence were often not allowed to testify in the actual courts.

The period of witchcraft hysteria was among the most tragic in history. Huge numbers of people were subjected to the most inhumane of tortures. A vast number of people were convicted of something that was at best nebulous, and a great many of these were executed. It was indeed a case of the slaughter of the innocents and a blot on the history of Europe and, in some cases, on that of the American colonies.

Chapter 3

Witches and Magicians:
The Accused and Self-Confessed

Aberdeen Witches

This was the name given to a group of people accused of witchcraft in the Aberdeen area in 1596–97. Most of the accused were elderly women and included Janet Wishart (page 197), Isobel Cockie (page 116), Margaret Ogg (page 166) and Helen Rogie (page 172). They were accused of a number of crimes that were regarded as a traditional part of witchcraft. These included causing death by witchcraft, harming people and livestock, turning milk sour and raising storms. In addition they were charged with cavorting with the devil and his demons and with indulging in lewd behaviour with them.

The scale of the witch-hunt and subsequent trials amounted to widespread hysteria and the trials were noted for their severity, twenty-four people being executed.

See Chapter 2, Aberdeen Witchcraft Trials, page 37.

Abramelin the Mage

A native of Würzburg in Germany, Abramelin (1362–1460) is now best known for the influence that he has had on other magicians and witches through the ages. He claimed to have been instructed how to conjure up demons and make them do his bidding and also how to raise storms. He also claimed that those who instructed him in these arts were none other than angels. It was his theory that everything in the world was the work of demons working under the instructions of angels and that each person had both an angel and a demon as a familiar.

Details of Abramelin's magic is said to be found in a manuscript written in French in the eighteenth century but claiming to be a translation of an original manuscript composed by Abramelin in Hebrew and dated 1458. It was translated into English as *The Sacred Magic of Abramelin the Mage* by S. L. MacGregor Mathers around the beginning of the twentieth century. Abramelin's work is said to have greatly influenced Aleister Crowley (page 122).

Isobel Adam

One of the Pittenweem Witches, named by Beatrice Laing (page 154) as a fellow-witch in her confession, Adam then confessed herself and spoke of selling her soul to the devil for wealth, having encountered him in Laing's house. She also confessed to having been involved with other witches, whom she named, in strangling a man. Despite this, she did not suffer the terrible fate of other witches, both supposed and self-confessed. Clearly she had connections with someone in authority because she was allowed to go free on payment of a small fine.

Agrippa

Agrippa (1496–1535), short for Henry Cornelius Agrippa von Nettesheim, is best known now for the influence that he has had on later followers of the occult. He was originally interested in knowledge generally and was a great scholar but he soon developed a particular fascination for alchemy and magic. He conducted extensive research into the state of the occult at that time and summed it up in *De Occulta Philosphia* (*On Occult Philosophy*, although this was not published until twenty years later).

Many people associate witchcraft, magic and the occult generally with the devil but Agrippa did not do so. It was his contention that the gift of magic was dependent on naturally occurring psychic gifts and he believed firmly that the mind had ascendancy over the body.

Agrippa had a chequered career, partly because of his beliefs but also because of his hot temper, and he had a succession of jobs throughout Europe, usually ending in disaster. People's suspicions of his beliefs hardened when he successfully defended a woman in Metz accused of witchcraft seemingly on the sole grounds that her mother had been burned as a witch. He won the case but gained a few more enemies and a reputation for being a supporter of witches. It was rumoured that he, himself, was a witch.

Various stories surround Agrippa. He is said to have been always accompanied by a black dog, which was widely taken to be his familiar. It is alleged that he had the ability to raise demons and that on one occasion he conjured up the spirit of the famous orator Tully to give a speech for him.

The charm of magic wore off as far as Agrippa was concerned. By the time of the publication of his book on the occult, written twenty years earlier, he had become disillusioned with magic and had turned to theology instead. After more unfortunate adventures, more quarrels with people and more wandering, he died in greenbelt in 1535. It is said that on his deathbed he renounced all his work on magic and attributed the many misfortunes in his life to this work.

Albertus Magnus

Born in Swabia in Germany, Albertus Magnus (1193?–1280) was a Dominican theologian and scholar who believed not in black magic but in the good magic that is naturally associated with nature, with plants, precious stones, etc. He was also a firm believer in the possibility of turning base metals into gold and wrote a book on alchemy.

There are many legends associated with Albertus Magnus. In one of the most famous he is credited with creating an android in the form of a man and with the gift of speech. The android, supposedly created using natural magic with some help from astrology, became his servant.

Albertus Magnus was a philosopher and a theologian. For his services to religion he was beatified in 1622 and canonised in 1932.

Alphonsus de Spina

A Spanish Franciscan monk who died in 1491, he was the author of the earliest work to be published on witches.

Charles Arnold

Arnold is noted for being the prime mover in getting Wicca, or witchcraft, legally recognised in Canada in December 1987. This was the result of lengthy negotiations, which began in April 1986 when Arnold applied unsuccessfully to his employers, the Humber College of Applied Arts and Technology, for leave at the Wiccan festivals of Beltane, celebrated on 1 May, and Samhain, celebrated on 31 October.

Arnold was born in Washington DC in 1947 and moved to Canada after his discharge from the US army, having served in Vietnam. He began practising witchcraft in the late 1970s.

Anne Baites

One of the Morpeth Witches who, with Anne Forster (page 129), was accused of attending sabbats. The main accuser, Anne Armstrong, claimed to have seen Baites take on various animal shapes, such as that of a cat and that of a hare, in rapid succession for the entertainment of the devil at one of the sabbats. She pleaded not guilty to this and other charges.

The trials of the Morpeth Witches are not very conclusive but it seems likely that they were acquitted and did not suffer the horrific fate of others accused of witchcraft.

Bamberg Witches

Some of the worst of the hysteria surrounding witchcraft in the sixteenth and seventeenth centuries occurred in Germany. Some of the worst hysteria and consequent witch-hunts and trials occurred in the small state of Bamberg (*see* Chapter 2, Bamberg Trials, page 30), especially during the rule of Prince-Bishop Gottfried Johann George II Fuchs.

A huge number of people were accused of witchcraft and found guilty on the flimsiest of supposed evidence at the most perfunctory of trials. Terror reigned and many more would have been accused, found guilty and executed had they not fled the country. Many prominent and wealthy citizens were among those accused of being Bamberg Witches. It was in the interests of the accusers and the state to accuse the wealthy because money was deducted from the estates of those found guilty to defray the cost of their trials, tortures and executions, while the residue went to the ruler-bishop.

One of the best remembered victims of the Bamberg witch mania was the Vice-Chancellor of Bamberg, George Hahn (page 149), who was so horrified by the slaughter going on around him that he felt compelled to protest. This action led to his own conviction for witchcraft and his forced confession implicated other local dignitaries.

Margaret Barclay

Most women accused of witchcraft were elderly but Margaret Barclay, who lived in Irvine in Ayrshire in the early seventeenth century, was a young woman. She was originally accused not of witchcraft but of theft, the charge being made by her brother-in-law, John Deans. The charges were unfounded, a fact verified by the church court, and, although things seemed to have been smoothed over, Barclay remained extremely annoyed about the whole affair.

When she heard that her brother-in-law was about to set off on a voyage as captain of a merchant vessel, people claimed that they heard her say that she wished that the ship might sink with the captain in it. Unfortunately for Margaret, the ship failed to return to shore at the time it was expected and rumours started. Now people said that she had been seen throwing pieces of hot coal into the sea, which piece of magic was meant to make the ship run aground. At this point a beggar, John Stewart (page 185), supposedly endowed with the gift of clairvoyance, stated that he had discovered by means of this gift that the ship was lost. When factual verification of this was made and the ship was found to have sunk off Cornwall, Stewart was arrested.

He immediately pointed the finger of suspicion at Barclay and at two other women whom he claimed were her accomplices, the women being Isobel Insh (page 152) and Isobel Crawford (page 121). In an effort to save himself, he told the authorities that he had been asked by Barclay to provide her with a curse that would have the effect of bringing destruction to the vessel. He further claimed that he knew that Barclay and her accomplices had met together to make clay figures of John Deans and some of his fellow sailors, this being a favourite charge against supposed witches, and had thrown them into the sea with a view to causing the men's ship to founder. On receiving the clay figures the sea had become very stormy and had turned red.

On hearing this perceived damning evidence, the authorities ordered Barclay to be arrested and set upon the process of making her confess. There were many horrific ways of dragging confessions from people accused of witchcraft (*see* Chapter 2, Witchcraft Trials), and it was Barclay's lot to have heavy iron bars placed on her legs until she could bear it no more and confessed to witchcraft. As was extremely common in the case of forced confessions, her confession was retracted after she had recovered slightly from the trauma of her torture. Her retraction was repeated in court but made no impression on the jury. She was found guilty, then first of all strangled and then burned at the stake.

Francis Barrett

The author of *Magus*, a book devoted to the occult and magic, published in London in 1801, Barrett was an eccentric who gave lessons in the art of magic. His book deals with such subjects as the natural magic inherent in plants and stones, alchemy, numerology and ceremonial magic, and had a significant influence on Eliphas Levi (page 155), a French occultist who did much to revive an interest in magic in the nineteenth century.

Elizabeth Barton

Known as the Maid of Kent, Elizabeth Barton (*c.* 1506–34) was a domestic servant who was accused of being a witch and of having committed treason after she made prophecies warning of a disaster that would befall Henry VIII after he divorced Anne Boleyn. This was clearly an unwise thing to do in respect of any monarch, let alone Henry VIII, and Barton paid the ultimate price by being condemned to death on charges of treason and being duly hanged at Tyburn.

Before her death she admitted that the prophecies were a piece of trumped-up deception and had no basis whatsoever. She laid the blame at the door of others who had got to hear of her supposed powers as a foreseer of the future and manipulated her for their own ends.

She acquired her fame as a prophet after making a seemingly amazing recovery from a series of violent fits at the chapel of a priest in Aldington in Kent. She claimed that her recovery was a gift from the Virgin Mary, who had also endowed her with the gift of prophecy. News of this spread, and people flocked to be told what she perceived their future to be. The chapel that was the scene of her recovery and the granting of her gift became a place of pilgrimage.

Naturally the priest of the chapel was delighted that his place of worship had become so famous. However, it was to emerge that his good fortune was far from accidental.

Barton's fits were simply pretence and it was the priest who had instructed her to fake them.

Barton was a naive serving girl and when she was feted by those wishing to profit from her supposed powers was flattered into making more and more false prophecies. Eventually her claims came to the notice of the king's critics and they thought to make use of her with a view to discrediting the king. Barton's succumbing to this particular piece of flattery cost her life.

Basque Witches *see* Pierre Bocal.

Elizabeth Bennet

One of the St Osyth Witches (page 173), Bennet was one of those accused by Ursula Kempe (page 152). She confessed to having two familiars, a creature resembling a dog, called Suckin, and one resembling a lion, called Lierd, and was charged with murder by means of witchcraft.

She was accused of having killed a farmer called William Byet because he had refused to sell her milk and had called her rude names. Furthermore, she was also accused of killing Byet's wife and two other people. Bennet was found guilty and executed by hanging.

Chatrina Blanckenstein

An elderly widow from Naumburg in Saxony, Chatrina Blanckenstein (1610–80) was accused of witchcraft. Her case, and later that of her daughter, serves to illustrate the fact that to be accused of witchcraft in the witch-obsessed years of the seventeenth century all you had to do was to be a woman and to be rather elderly.

Blanckenstein was accused of the murder of a child by

witchcraft. The hysteria surrounding witchcraft at that time was such that hardly any misfortune was held to occur naturally – it had to be laid at a witch's door. The old woman's only connection with the dead child was that her daughter, being short of fuel, had exchanged some of this for some jam made by her mother. The child ate this and died four years later. The child's parents promptly accused the Blanckenstein household of witchcraft.

There followed one of the commonest and saddest aspects of witchcraft charges. At the slightest suggestion of witchcraft previously friendly neighbours would accuse each other, seeking to add credence to their accusations by pointing to various occurrences or phenomena supposedly associated with witchcraft. They had seen a hare running from the scene, where dead livestock were found, towards the door of a particular neighbour, proving supposedly that the hare was the neighbour returning from killing the livestock by means of witchcraft. Or the neighbour was always seen with a black dog and this was bound to be the devil in disguise, her helper in her nefarious practices.

The things supposedly associated with witchcraft (*see* Chapter 4) were well known. It simply took an overactive imagination, a predisposition to hysteria, a spirit of revenge or ill-will towards a neighbour, or simply a desire to point the finger of suspicion at somebody else before it could be pointed at oneself for people to be convinced that there was a witch in their midst and to name her.

After the allegations by her fellow-villagers Blanckenstein was charged with infanticide by means of witchcraft. Despite protestations of total innocence, she was imprisoned and subjected to a range of the horrific tortures that were a regular part of witch trials (*see* Chapter 2, Witchcraft Trials). The very sight of some of the instruments of torture were enough to terrify some accused witches into confession but Blanckenstein remained adamant about her innocence even when the worst of these were applied to her. Finally, when she had somehow survived unbelievable torture, her tormentors let her go. In this she was fortunate because often they took the inability to be broken down by torture as a sign that the tortured person was being helped to sustain the pain by the devil.

The charges were dropped and she was released. However, she did not go scot-free. Ironically, she was forced to pay to the authorities the cost of her tortures.

This was not, alas, the end of the family's suffering. There was a deep-seated belief that witchcraft ran in families. The article on Agrippa, given on page 94, tells how he defended a woman in Metz on charges of witchcraft seemingly based solely on charges that her mother was burned as a witch. People were generally suspicion of the relatives of anyone who had been accused of witchcraft.

So it was that Blanckenstein's daughter suffered the cruel fate that her mother had avoided. In 1689, some years after her mother had died, the daughter was accused of being involved in the death of another baby. This time the authorities were determined not to let her go but, in any case, she was not made of such stern stuff as her mother and was moved to confess to charges of witchcraft at the sight of the torturing equipment that they proposed to use on her.

She confessed to being involved in the murder of the child and to various other charges relating to witchcraft, such as killing livestock and denying God and Christ. As was very frequently the case in forced confessions, she also named supposed accomplices. Having made her confession, she then tried to commit suicide by hanging herself by her belt in prison. Her tormentors were not to let her take such a way out, however, and they resuscitated her with the intention of making her death much more painful. They burned her alive, a common way to put witches to death.

John Blymire

Blymire was the central figure in a murder trial in York County, Pennsylvania, in January 1929. The case attracted a great deal of attention because it was widely held that the case had strong connections with witchcraft, although the authorities insisted that the motive for murder was robbery.

In the early part of the twentieth century there was still a strong belief in witchcraft in the York area of Pennsylvania. Blymire was born into a family of German extraction and many of its members were meant to have the power to heal and to bewitch people. Such powers were known locally as powwowing, after the North American Indian word for a ceremonial meeting for discussion.

As a boy Blymire appeared to be suffering from a wasting disease that neither his father or grandfather, noted witches and healers, could cure. Consequently he was taken to another witch, Nelson Rehmeyer, a few miles away, to be cured. A cure was duly effected and later Blymire was employed by Rehmeyer on his farm.

Gradually the young Blymire began to develop a reputation for his healing skills. He was not very bright, was physically unattractive and had few friends, but people began to seek him out as a healer and he had some spectacular success. Shortly after he had drawn attention to himself by stopping a mad dog in its tracks and curing it instantly of rabies, Blymire became ill and appeared once again to be suffering from a wasting disease.

Nothing seemed to go right for him, and Blymire, who was at that time still a youth, became obsessed with the notion that someone had put a spell on him. He gave up his job in a cigar factory and began to roam from place to place, taking short-term jobs and making some money from healing but all the while trying to find someone who could break the spell that he was convinced had been placed on him.

In 1917 he got married and for a while his health and luck appeared to improve. After the deaths in infancy of two of his children, however, his health took a turn for the worse and he lost his job. His obsession with the notion of a spell on him returned and he consulted yet more witches to find the source of his bewitchment. By this time he was suspecting everyone, including his wife, and a psychiatrist arranged for him to be admitted to mental hospital.

He was there for only a short time and in June 1928 he consulted another witch, one Nellie Noll, a very old woman whose powers were held in great regard. After a few sessions she told Blymire, whose wife by this time had divorced him, that she had succeeded in identifying the person who was at the centre of his misfortune. She named Rehmeyer, the healer who had cured Blymire as a boy and his ex-employer. Blymire at first was disinclined to believe this but was eventually convinced and vowed vengeance on Rehmeyer.

An important book in local witchcraft lore was *Powwows*, or *Long Lost Friend*, written by John Hohmar and containing suggested cures, spells, etc. Noll told her client that he could break the spell cast on him in one of two ways. He could cut a lock of his tormentor's hair and bury it deep in the ground or he could remove his copy of *Long Lost Friend* and bury it.

By this time Blymire had teamed up with a youth named John Curry, who blamed his unhappy childhood on a spell of unknown origin. They were now joined by Wilbert Hess, son of a farmer whose crops and livestock were in a poor way and who was convinced that this was also the result of a spell laid on him. The father had originally consulted Blymire professionally but he secretly consulted Noll on behalf of the Hess family and Curry. She again pointed the finger of suspicion at Nelson Rehmeyer.

Now it took a great deal of courage to confront Rehmeyer because he was a huge man with the reputation of being able to conjure up demons. After an unsuccessful visit, the three returned to Rehmeyer's house and demanded 'the book'. He claimed ignorance of what they were talking about. His attackers succeed in felling the huge man and in getting a rope round his neck to choke him. They then beat and kicked him to death. Before they left they ransacked his house for money but this amounted to very little.

The attackers were soon found and arrested, and Blymire was proud to proclaim his part in the murder of the person whom he claimed had put a spell on him and ruined his life. In most parts of America witchcraft was not an issue by this time and the press made the most of the stories of witchcraft. The judge in charge of the case, Ray Sherwood, did not want to have the area dubbed a backward place ruled by superstition and instructed the lawyers involved in the case that it would be dealt with as summarily as possible and that no mention of witchcraft was to be made in the course of the trial.

Instead of witchcraft, the official motive for the crime was to be robbery. This was not really credible, since the amount stolen was thought to be less than three dollars. Blymire's defence lawyers disagreed with the judge's ruling but were forced to go along with it. It was their feeling that Blymire stood a better chance with the jury, whose members were likely to share his belief in witchcraft, if his motive for murder could be shown to be witchcraft rather than robbery.

However, the official motive for murder remained robbery, and all three accused were found guilty of murder. Blymire and Curry were given life sentences and Hess twenty years. After serving nearly twenty-four years, Blymire was released at the age of fifty-six and returned to live in York.

Pierre Bocal

The Basque region of the Pyrenees was at several points in history considered to be a centre of witchcraft. When Christianity came to the region, which had tended to retain its own culture separate from the rest of France and Spain, the old beliefs concerning the old gods to some extent became entangled with the new beliefs. As in other parts of the world, the pagan beliefs exercised some influence on the new religion and in some cases the old beliefs lived alongside the new beliefs.

The Basque region in Spain received particular attention from the authorities during the time of the Spanish Inquisition (from around 1480). They were determined to root out witchcraft and, as was usually the case, where witchcraft was suspected ways and means were found to prove it, whether or not there was any actual objective evidence. The man in charge of the witch-hunt was a lawyer, Pierre de Lancre, and he was completely ruthless and obsessive

The assiduousness of the Spanish Inquisition in rooting out witchcraft in the Spanish Basque region had greatly impressed the French, and in the early seventeenth century, they set about doing the same in the French Basque region. Their commitment was, if anything, greater than the Spanish, and their activity amounted to slaughter. There was the usual series of tortures and forced confessions and invitations to some to implicate neighbours in order to achieve immunity for themselves. Many children were involved in reporting that they had seen relatives and neighbours flying through the air, working spells, etc. Huge numbers of people were alleged to be attending sabbats, or gatherings of witches arranged in order to reaffirm allegiance to the devil and to indulge in orgies of an obscene nature.

Best known among the victim's of de Lancre's excesses was a young priest who was accused of witchcraft because it was rumoured that he officiated not only over Christian rites but over pagan rites, the pagan element in religion still being very much in evidence in the Basque region. When he was found wearing a goat's-head mask at a pagan ceremony, he was assumed to be involved in witchcraft and was burned alive. The people were shocked that such treatment had been meted out to a priest, and one so young – he was twenty-seven.

Three more priests were burned and the slaughter of others continued. Eventually the local populace were shocked into protest and went on the rampage. De Lancre was forced to give up his terrible witch-hunts.

Christine Boffgen

A native of Rheinbach, a village in Germany, Boffgen was one of the most famous victims of Franz Buirmann, who acted as a kind of itinerant judge at witchcraft trials and who was notorious for the severity of his tortures. As was often the case with those accused of witchcraft, the person at the heart of the charges, namely Boffgen, was an elderly woman, and a very respected one at that.

Her accusers were people who were already in jail on charges of witchcraft, it being very common for those making forced confessions to implicate other people who were quite innocent, as indeed they themselves probably were. First she was blindfolded and shaved and was then subjected to a series of the most cruel tortures routinely used in witchcraft trials (*see* Chapter 2, Witchcraft Trials). In particular, she was subjected to the use of boots, vises designed to enclose the legs of the accused that were then tightened until the bones of the legs were crushed and the flesh torn. One can only guess at the scale of the agony endured by people subjected to this heinous torture and sympathise with the wretches who confessed to crimes that they had never committed and to connections with a way of life that they had never had just to stop the excruciating pain.

With the worst of the pain abated, many of the accused came to enough of their senses to realise that agony had forced them into false confessions and they recanted. This is what happened in the case of Boffgen. However, her tormentors did not accept this and simply ordered more physical torture. By this time her body was too weak to sustain any more punishment and after four days of it she died in 1631.

Great shame was felt in the village and the sense of shame was to last for an extremely long time. As recently as the early part of the twentieth century, masses were still being said for her in the local church.

Raymond Buckland

Born in England in 1934, Buckland went to live in America in 1962 and is credited with having done much to introduce contemporary witchcraft there. His father was of gypsy blood and one of his uncles interested him in spiritualism from an early age. He then went on to develop an interest in the occult and witchcraft.

He was greatly influenced by *Witchcraft Today* by Gerald Gardner (page 132) with whom he corresponded regularly while establishing a coven. The two men met in 1964, after Buckland's initiation into witchcraft. Later he turned his back on some of Gardner's teachings and formed a new tradition of witchcraft with Saxon connections, known as Seaxa-Wica. He has written extensively on witchcraft.

George Burroughs

One of the Salem Witches (page 174, *see also* Salem trials, page 41), Burroughs had been parish minister at Salem from 1680 until 1682. The Putnam family were hostile to Burroughs since he had formerly been their lodger and had fallen out with them. By this time he was a resident of Wells, Maine, but he was accused and brought to Salem on the grounds that he had asked some of the girls to sign devil's pacts. His spectre was accused of biting the girls and Tituba (page 185) accused him of being head of a coven to which she belonged. In addition, he was accused of murder. He absolutely refused to accept that there was such a thing as witchcraft and was found guilty and hanged with John Proctor (page 171) on 19 August 1692. Even the fact that he was able to say the Lord's Prayer (page 76) just before his death did not save him, although witches were not meant to be able to do this. Some of the crowd grew restive but they were persuaded that Burroughs was indeed a witch and in any case would have been too terrified to try to prevent the execution for fear of reprisals.

Chelmsford Witches

Chelmsford in Essex was the centre of much witchcraft hysteria from the mid-sixteenth century until about a century later. The first person executed (July 1566) under the tenets of the Witchcraft Act, passed in 1563, was an alleged Chelmsford witch. This was Agnes Waterhouse (page 191). Also accused of witchcraft in Chelmsford were Joan Waterhouse (page 192), daughter of Agnes, and Elizabeth Francis (page 130).

Another wave of witchcraft hysteria hit Chelmsford in 1579. Elizabeth Francis was again involved in this, as were Ellen Smith (page 183), Alice Nokes (page 163) and Margery Stanton.

This was far from being the end of Chelmsford's association with witch trials. In 1582 it was the venue of the trial of the St Osyth Witches and in 1589 nine women and one man were put on trial. Several charges of murder were made and many of the witnesses for the prosecution were children. Of the ten accused, four were executed and three of them went to the gallows within two hours of a guilty verdict having been reached. The three were Joan Cony, Joan Prentice and Joan Upney, and in the last hour before they were hanged all three confessed to the crimes of which they had been tried, although they had denied them up until then. Doubtless this was an attempt to be shown clemency or granted a pardon but the attempt was in vain.

In 1610 Chelmsford was again to be the scene of another witch trial. This time the accused was Katherine Lawrett from Colne Wake in Essex. Harm done to animals by means of witchcraft was a common charge and such was the nature of the accusation made against Lawrett. She was charged with having used her supposed magic to bring about the death of a valuable horse belonging to a man called Francis Plaite.

Chelmsford's association came to prominence again in 1645. That year saw the start of a notorious mass trial, thirty-two women being put on trial in July. Five of these were named by the first of these supposed witches to be questioned and tortured, Elizabeth Clarke (page 113) of Manningtree. These five in turn named others, and so it went on. It was an unfortunate aspect of witch trials that once someone was arrested he or she seemed only to eager to implicate others, perhaps in an attempt to curry favour with, and so receive clemency from, the authorities or perhaps from a determination not to suffer alone.

Seventeen of the accused were hanged, one of these being Clarke, two were acquitted and various fates befell the others. The trial was notorious for the methods used to obtain confessions, these including depriving the accused of sleep for days at a time, forcing them to walk back and forwards continuously until they fell down with exhaustion, compelling them to sit cross-legged on a stool for hours at a time and submitting them to the swimming test. This last involved throwing the accused into a stretch of water, such as a pond or river, having first bound him or her hand and foot. If the accused person floated then it was assumed that help was being given by the devil and the person was deemed to be guilty of witchcraft. If the person sank then innocence was assumed but this was often of small comfort since the person often drowned.

Organising the initial proceedings that led to these trials was the notorious witch-finder Matthew Hopkins, totally relentless in his efforts to identify, prosecute and execute anyone supposedly associated with witchcraft. It is likely that his attitude affected that of the trial judges (*see* Chapter 2, Chelmsford Witchcraft Trials, page 33).

Elizabeth Clarke

One of the Chelmsford Witches (page 111), Clarke was tried during the fourth wave of witch trials to be held in Chelmsford. The trials took place in 1645 and were largely at the instigation of the notorious witch-finder Matthew Hopkins, who called himself Witch-finder General. They were noted for the extremity of the torture used to extract confessions.

Clarke was the first of this series of accused witches to be charged. She was an elderly woman, which alone made her a prime target for being accused of witchcraft. She also had only one leg and was rather strange-looking, which confirmed her status as prime target. Finally, as if she needed any other factors against her, she was the daughter of a convicted witch – and a hanged witch at that.

Hopkins the witch-finder was exceptionally eager to find supposed evidence against anyone accused of witchcraft and claimed that he had seen various of Clarke's supposed familiars in various shapes, including a legless spaniel called Jarmara and a polecat called Newes. The old woman confessed to having a series of familiars, after having been tortured, and also confessed to having had intercourse with the devil over a period of several years. Given the severity of the tortures that were associated with the 1645 Chelmsford trials, it is hardly surprising that Clarke confessed. She was found guilty and hanged.

Elizabeth Clauson

One of the Stamford Witches (page 183), Clauson was the first to be accused. She was an extremely well-respected person in the community and it was a great surprise to everyone when Katherine Branch, a servant girl, accused the woman of being the cause of the fits and visions from which she was suffering. However, she and Branch's employer's wife, Mrs Westwood, had been involved in a long-term quarrel over some flax and there could have been an element of revenge in the girl's claim.

Other people were also accused, principally Mercy Disborough (page 123). Clauson and Disborough and three others were made the subject of a court of inquiry in May 1692.

Apparently Mrs Westwood felt that her servant might well be lying but she was powerless to do anything. On being searched for evidence of the devil's mark, by which the devil was supposed to imprint those who had vowed allegiance to him, Clauson was found to have only a wart, which was deemed to be harmless. Meanwhile the servant girl continued to have regular fits.

Clauson and Disborough were imprisoned and the trial began in September. Disborough insisted on being subjected to the swimming test to prove her innocence and Clauson also had to undertake it. This was an ordeal, common elsewhere but not in America, involving a suspected witch being bound hand and foot and thrown into a stretch of water, such as a pond or river, to see if he or she would float or sink. If the accused floated, it was deemed to be a sign of guilt, and if he or she sank it was a sign of innocence, although it was also often a cause of death.

Both women survived and were thus deemed to be guilty of witchcraft. Numerous people were found to testify against Clauson but at first no one could be found to testify in her favour. This was not surprising, as people giving testimony on behalf of an accused witch were liable to be accused of witchcraft themselves and charged with being accomplices.

Such was Clauson's standing in the community, however, that two of her neighbours risked the wrath of the court and did indeed testify in her favour. Perhaps thinking that there was safety in numbers, others then followed suit, and soon seventy-six of the townspeople had indicated that they were willing to testify as to Clauson's character and conduct.

In the light of this, the jury felt unable to reach a verdict and five ministers were called in to investigate the evidence that had been taken in the course of the trial and also the trial records. As has been mentioned above, the ordeal of swimming as a test for witchcraft was not usually used in America, and the ministers decided to disallow the evidence deduced from it, saying that the test was not only illegal but sinful. In addition they suggested that Branch might either be guilty of deception or have inherited a physical condition from which her mother had suffered.

The court was reconvened in October and further testimony was put forward. By this time the Salem witchcraft trials were at their height. Clauson was found not guilty and was set free. She died in Stamford in 1714 at the age of eighty-three. The Stamford trials were conducted with considerably more restraint than those at Salem.

Isobel Cockie

One of the supposed witches involved in the witch trials in Aberdeen in 1596 (pages 37, 93). She was accused of putting a spell on livestock so that they failed to produce milk, lay eggs, etc. Such a charge was very common among those seeking to charge someone with witchcraft.

Cologne Witches

Germany in the seventeenth century was the scene of much witchcraft hysteria and of relentless witch-hunts and cruel tortures. Cologne was by no means one of the worst areas and indeed had a reputation for enlightenment. However, there were two periods when Cologne was affected by witch mania, one between 1625 and 1626 and another between 1630 and 1636, but even then the authorities were disposed to be lenient.

Several witches were put on trial during the first of these periods. Of these Cologne Witches the most discussed was Catherine Henot (page 151). She was accused of putting a spell on some of the nuns of the St Clare order. Around 1929 many people were accused of witchcraft by Christine Plum, who claimed to have been possessed by demons conjured up by the accused.

Yet more people were accused of witchcraft after 1631 when there was an exodus of inhabitants from Leipzig to Cologne after their native city became caught up in a war with Sweden. This had an unfortunate effect on Cologne since Leipzig had had a great number of witch-hunters, dedicated to rooting out witchcraft, and these turned their attention to their new home city. Many people were accused of witchcraft and prosecuted, the situation only calming down in 1636 after papal intervention.

The last witch to be executed according to official records was killed in 1655.

Connecticut Witches

The title refers to a number of people accused of witchcraft throughout the northeastern part of America around the period 1647–62. New England had recently been settled and the settlers were much influenced by the mores of their mother country, England. Part of this influence took the form of an attitude to witchcraft that bordered on paranoia and hysteria. In 1642 legislation against witchcraft was passed in Connecticut, and this led to several executions. *See* Rebecca Greensmith (page 146), Katherine Harrison (page 151), Mary Johnson (page 152), Mary Parsons (page 166), Alice Young (page 200).

Mrs Corbyn

Known as the Fressingfield Witch, Corbyn had the distinction of being accused of witchcraft after her death. She died on the day in 1890 that also saw the death of a child to whom she was step-grandmother. Corbyn is said to have announced on her deathbed that she felt that the child was not likely to out-live her for long.

At the inquest into the sudden death of the child, the medical examiner gave the opinion that the child had died of shock, this having been in response to the application of some kind of irritant that could not be identified. Immedi-ately the child's parents claimed that the child's death was the result of witchcraft practised by Corbyn. The dead woman's husband then said that he had always had the sus-picion that his wife was a witch and had been scared to an-noy her throughout their married life lest she use her black art to harm him.

Giles Corey

One of the Salem Witches (page 174), Giles Corey was the husband of Martha Corey (page 119) and he had thought her guilty of witchcraft. When he himself, as an old man of eighty, was accused of witchcraft he refused to plead to the charge. It is thought that he did so because he knew that the property of convicted witches was confiscated by the Crown and because he believed that his property could not be confiscated if he refused to plead and so could not be convicted.

His case is unique in America in that physical torture was used on him and he was pressed to death despite the act of 1641 that forbade inhuman or cruel punishment. Furious that he would not speak, the authorities forced him to lie on the ground with a large wooden plank covering him. Heavy boulders were then placed at intervals on the plank with a view to forcing him to beg for mercy and plead guilty – or even to plead at all. However, he somehow withstood the terrible torture for two days and then died.

Martha Corey

One of the Salem Witches (page 174), Martha Corey was an upstanding member of the community and a pious church member, but this did not save her from the hysterical claims of the girls who claimed that her spectre regularly attacked them. They put up such a convincing show that even Martha Corey's husband, local landowner Giles Corey (page 118), thought her guilty of witchcraft. She was found guilty and hanged on 22 September 1692.

Janet Cornfoot

One of the Pittenweem Witches, Cornfoot was named by Beatrice Laing (page 154) as a fellow-witch in her confession, confessed after torture and withdrew the confession after recovering from the distress of the torture. She was locked up in a steeple rather than in the gaol because the authorities were worried that she would persuade other inmates of the gaol who had confessed to witchcraft to withdraw their confessions.

She succeeded in escaping from the steeple and sought help and shelter from the local minister, Patrick Cowper, not being aware of the fact that he had been instrumental in getting the charge of witchcraft brought against Laing in the first place. He was very much concerned in stamping out witchcraft, so was quite the wrong person to ask for help. She had no choice but to seek refuge in the house of someone who was a suspected witch.

This simply exacerbated the situation, and she was set

upon by an angry mob early in 1705 and severely beaten. Worse, the mob strung a rope between a ship and the shore and hanged her from it so that they could pelt her with stones. Following this they took her down and submitted her to a terrible death by covering her with a heavy door and piling boulders on this until she was crushed to death.

As was often the case with the kind of agonising deaths suffered by witches, no punitive action was taken against the perpetrators. The authorities simply turned a blind eye, glad to be rid of another supposed witch.

Mrs Julian Cox

A beggarwoman, she was charged with witchcraft and tried at Taunton in Somerset in 1663. Her accuser was a servant girl who accused Cox of putting a spell on her after she refused to give her any money. Revenge was often put forward as a motive for someone practising witchcraft on another.

Cox was accused of a number of activities traditionally associated with witchcraft. She was charged with putting a spell on a neighbour's livestock in order to harm them, in particular with putting a spell on a neighbour's cows to drive them mad. She was also charged with flying around on a broomstick, a traditional form of transport for witches, and was supposedly seen flying in through her own window on it. It was traditional for a witch to have a familiar and Cox was said to keep a pet toad.

Cox was claimed to be particularly skilled at shape-changing, another common activity supposedly associated with witches. In particular she had a reputation for turning herself into a hare. One person who accused her of such an ability claimed that his hounds had chased a hare into a large bush.

When he tried to get at the hare, the creature vanished and its place stood a woman whom he instantly identified as Cox. He was absolutely terrified but was able to ask her how she came to be in the bush. He reported that the woman was so out of breath that she could not answer him, and this led him to suppose that this breathlessness was a result of being chased by his hounds in the shape of a hare.

The accused did not do her case any good by claiming that she herself had seen two witches and a black man, presumed to be the devil, flying low to the ground on broomsticks.

One of the more lenient ways of trying supposed witches was to get them to say the Lord's Prayer (page 76). If they could not, or made any mistake, this was seen as evidence of consorting with the devil and so of witchcraft. Cox almost passed the test. She made one serious mistake, however, that proved fatal. In the line from the Lord's Prayer 'And lead us not into temptation' she omitted the word 'not'. This was taken as definite evidence of guilt rather than just an unfortunate accidental slip, and she was found guilty and executed. On such tenuous evidence were many witches sent to their deaths.

Isobel Crawford

One of the alleged accomplices of Margaret Barclay (page 98), Crawford was named as an accomplice both by Barclay in her forced confession, it being a common practice among people being tortured to try to get a confession out of them to implicate others, and by John Stewart (page 185). She protested her innocence vehemently but in vain. Even after being subjected to horrific torture she refused to confess to witchcraft and was burnt at the stake.

Aleister Crowley

A British occultist, Crowley was born in 1875 into a family of Plymouth Brethren, a strict religious sect, and he appears to have rebelled against his strict upbringing at an early age. He became interested in the occult and devoted more time to his study of this at the University of Cambridge than to his conventional studies, being influenced by a book entitled *The Book of Black Magic and of Pacts*, written by Arthur Edward Waite.

Leaving Cambridge without graduating, he became a member of the Hermetic Order of the Golden Dawn, a society devoted to the study of the occult, led by Samuel Liddell. However, Crowley was determined to achieve greatness, fell out with Liddell, with whom he then conducted a feud, and was expelled from the group. Crowley then travelled widely to learn more about the occult and mysticism.

In Egypt he supposedly had communications with a spirit called Aiwass. Allegedly the spirit was endowed with a voice and dictated to Crowley the information that was to form his most famous book, *The Book of the Law*, which contains the law 'Do what thou wilt shall be the only law'. Aiwass apparently also announced the dawning of new age, the Age of Horus, of which Crowley was the prophet.

Crowley has been variously hailed as a renowned magician who achieved great feats and as a man of great wickedness. His reputation as a magician was much marred for many by his sexual excesses, which were associated both with his person relationships and his magic rituals. He had become involved with a German occult movement, called the Order of the Temple of the Orient, which practised sex magic, and his interest in this grew.

He moved to America in 1915 and lived there until 1919, after which he went to Sicily and founded the Abbey of Thelema, which he hoped to make an international centre for occult studies. However, stories of his sex ceremonies spread and he was ordered to leave Sicily. He took to his travels again, became addicted to heroin and fell into financial difficulties. He eventually died in England in 1947.

Dalkeith Witch *see* Christine WILSON.

Madeleine Demandolx *see* Louis GAUFRIDI.

Elizabeth Device

One of the Pendle Witches (page 166).

Mercy Disborough

One of the Stamford Witches, Disborough, with Elizabeth Clauson (page 114), was one of the main accused, having had the finger of suspicion pointed at her by Katherine Branch, a servant girl who blamed her fits and visions on witchcraft practised by some of the women in the town. With Clauson, she was searched for evidence of the devil's mark. In the case of Disborough, the searchers claimed success, saying that they had found unnatural marks that qualified as devil's marks.

Disborough was duly charged and brought to trial, the trial opening on 14 September 1692. Although such a test for witchcraft was uncommon in America, but usual elsewhere, Disborough asked for the swimming test to be applied. This test involved binding the accused hand and foot and casting him or her into a stretch of water. If the accused floated, then guilt was assumed, it being supposed that witchcraft had come to his or her aid. On the other hand, sinking was thought to be a sign of innocence, although this presumed innocence was often paid for by the accused's death from drowning.

Disborough and Clauson both floated and were thus found to be guilty of witchcraft. However, partly because a great number of people came forward to testify to the good character and conduct of Disborough's co-accused, Clauson, the trial jury, after long deliberation, found themselves unable to reach a verdict.

A committee consisting of five ministers was called in to review the evidence that had been given in the course of the trial and also to review the trial records. They decided to disallow the results of the swimming test, deeming it to be both unlawful and sinful. They also disallowed the evidence supplied by Disborough's supposed devil's marks, unless the marks that had been found on her skin should be so described by a competent physician after investigation. The five ministers also cast doubt on Branch's allegations by suggesting that she might be guilty of deception or that she might be suffering from the same physical condition from which her mother had suffered.

The court was reconvened on 28 October and more evidence was heard. This time the jury found Disborough guilty and she was sentenced to death, although her co-accused, Clauson, was found not guilty and released. In the end Disborough's execution did not take place. After the trial her friends made application to the court that the second session of the court was not lawful in light of the fact that one of the original jurors was not present. She was reprieved, thus having her life saved by a technicality.

Gilly Duncan

The woman who sparked off the witchcraft trial surrounding the North Berwick Witches (page 163) of 1590–92, Duncan was a servant girl in the employment of an local dignitary, David Seaton, in the town of Tranent in East Lothian near Edinburgh. He became suspicious of her when she began to be involved in healing people, his assumption being that these skills were inspired by the devil rather than God. His suspicions deepened when it came to his attention that she was leaving the house at night on mysterious nocturnal visits.

Seaton had legal authority, being a deputy bailiff, and he took it upon himself to exert his official powers in his own home. Not only did he exercise his powers of questioning but he exercised extremely painful forms of torture on the girl. He is said to have made use of the process known as thrawing, in which the accused's head was jerked violently by a rope. This would obviously have been extremely painful, and it was followed by use of the 'pilliwinks' or thumbscrews. This instrument of torture consisted of a vice in which the thumbs of suspects were crushed, and it is a testament to the severity of the other forms of torture used in witchcraft trials that this was considered one of the less severe tortures.

These tortures having been carried out, Duncan was then subjected to a body search for signs of the devil's mark with which the devil was meant to imprint in various ways, such as by touching or kissing the bodies of those who promised to serve him. It could be in any part of the body and the search for it was often humiliating. Also, since hardly anyone has a flawless body, a great many naturally occurring marks were said to be proof of the devil's involvement.

This being the case, it was not surprising that a devil's mark was supposedly found on Duncan's body – on her throat. After the finding of the devil's mark and after enduring the various tortures, Duncan had had enough and agreed to give a formal confession admitting to an association with witchcraft and the devil. She was determined not to go down alone, however, and set about implicating other people. This was an extremely common feature of witchcraft trials. It may have been the result of not wishing to face something alone, it may have been an act of vengeance or it may have been a result of a belief that naming accomplices would involve the accused being treated more leniently.

Whatever the reason, Duncan provided a significant list of people who had shared her involvement in witchcraft. These included Agnes Sampson (page 175), whose revelations in the trial, including efforts to bring about the death of the king, King James I of Scotland, were so sensational that many people disbelieved them, two women of noble connections, Effie Maclean (page 157) and Barbara Napier (page 163), and John Fian (page 127), a schoolteacher.

Susanna Edwards

One of the Exeter Witches (page 127) who voluntarily confessed to witchcraft and were hanged in 1682. Edwards, who in common with her co-accused, Temperance Lloyd (page 156) and Mary Trembles (page 187), was impoverished and elderly, openly claimed to have been recruited to witchcraft by the devil himself.

In the course of her trial she shocked the people attending it by her account of her meeting with the devil, who had taken on the guise of a gentleman dressed in black. She is said to have given independent evidence of her guilt by glaring at her guard in jail until he fell down in a fit. She was found guilty with the others and they were hanged in August 1682.

Exeter Witches

The Exeter witches consisted of Susanna Edwards (page 126), Temperance Lloyd (page 156) and Mary Trembles (page 187). Their trial for suspected witchcraft in Bideford in 1682 was one of the last major witchcraft trials to be conducted in England.

The women, all poor, elderly and often seeming confused were accused of belonging to a coven. Their actions did not help their case. All three women gave voluntary confessions of such a shocking nature that the people of Exeter were virtually baying for their blood. As was often the case with witchcraft trials, the start of the case saw several people bringing charges against the accused, although these had never been mentioned before. These charges, as was not unusual, were vague in the extreme, one of them being based on the fact that someone had claimed to have seen a cat jump in at the window and had assumed it to be the devil.

It is said that the judge felt quite sorry for the women but, in the light of public opinion against them, he could take no other course of action than to find them guilty. They were duly sentenced to death and hanged in August 1682.

John Fian

Mostly it was women who were accused of witchcraft but Fian was an exception. A respected schoolmaster, he was one of the people accused of belonging to a coven known as the

North Berwick Witches. He was one of those whom Gilly Duncan (page 125) named as one of her accomplices when she confessed to witchcraft. Fian was found guilty and put to death by strangling and burning at the stake.

Dietrich Flade

A civil judge appointed to officiate at the wholesale trials of the Trèves Witches (page 187), he was accused of leniency in his judgements and dismissed from his post. Later he himself was accused of witchcraft, found guilty and executed.

Joan Flower

An English peasant who was unusual among women accused of witchcraft in that she admitted to some of the charges without torture, although she later retracted the confession before her death in 1618. Flower had been widely suspected of being a witch for some considerable time before she was tried and was also considered to be a particularly unpleasant person.

The events that led to her being charged began when one of her daughters, Margaret, who worked as chief laundress at Belvoir Castle, home of Francis, sixth earl of Rutland, was dismissed on charges of stealing food and of staying out at night. The outraged Margaret immediately sought her mother's help in seeking vengeance.

The mother first rather foolishly cursed the earl in public. She then asked her other daughter, Philippa, who worked as an occasional cleaner at the castle to try to obtain some of the personal possessions of the earl's family. In this way she is alleged to have obtained a glove belonging to the earl's eldest son, Henry, and to have used her magic to treat it in various ways before burying it. This was supposedly done in order to bring misfortune to the owner of the glove. Henry died a few years later and his two surviving brothers became ill, supposedly after Flower had subjected them to similar magical feats.

These and other misfortunes that befell the earl and his family reminded some local people of the curse that Flower had put on the earl and witchcraft was suspected. These suspicions were strengthened by the fact that Flower and her daughters did not try to conceal that they had plotted for the undoing of the earl's family. They were duly arrested and were committed for trial in the company of others accused of being accomplices. During the trial they admitted to being members of a coven and confessed to other misdeeds associated with witchcraft.

Too late did Flower realise where their confessions were leading. Not wishing to be executed, she is said to have retracted any confession of association with witchcraft and to have declared her innocence. It is said that she reached for a piece of dry bread and put it in her mouth, declaiming that the bread might choke her if she were guilty of the charges. Alas for her – she choked to death in front of the judges of the court. It was unfortunate also for her daughters. Not only did they lose their mother but the seeming proof of her guilt led the judges to declare them and their co-accused guilty also and they were hanged in Lincoln in March 1619.

Anne Forster

The main suspect at the heart of witchcraft trials in Morpeth in 1673, Forster was accused by Anne Armstrong, a local servant girl. Armstrong claimed that she had been forced to carry Forster to a sabbat, an orgiastic gathering of witches, the woman having supposedly having put a bridle over Armstrong's head, this being a popular part of witchcraft lore. Having been put under a spell so that she was devoid of will she was forced to carry her load cross-legged to the sabbat.

Later she was forced to carry other members of the coven to sabbats. Her supposed attendance at the sabbats gave her ample opportunity to recognise and name more people whom she claimed to be present. Armstrong went into great detail about the activities of the witches at the sabbats, claiming that there were several covens present and a long black man on horseback whom she took to be the devil.

As well as accusing Forster of attending sabbats, Armstrong claimed that she had performed a number of misdeeds associated with witchcraft, such as using her black art to put spells on the livestock belonging to anyone whom she disliked. Accusing people of deeds linked to witchcraft often seems to have created a chain reaction, and soon others followed Armstrong's example, Forster being accused, among other things, of bringing about the death of a neighbour's child.

Three of the other people accused with Forster were Anne Baites (page 97), Dorothy Green (page 146) and Mary Hunter. They all denied the charges, and although the trial records do not shed much light on the case it is likely that the trial was a great deal milder than many witch trials. It is likely that all the accused were acquitted, although two of the supposed coven spent some time in prison.

Elizabeth Francis

One of the early Chelmsford Witches, Francis was accused at

the same time as Agnes Waterhouse and her daughter, Joan, in 1566. Like the Waterhouses, she was a resident of Hatfield Peverel in Essex, and in fact, although the charges against Francis and the Waterhouses were quite separate, there was a connection between them relating to the details of the trial. The cat, known as Sathan, which at time of her trial was owned by Agnes Waterhouse and which was accused of being her familiar and accomplice, had once been owned by Francis and had been given by her to Waterhouse. Indeed the cat's ownership was even more complicated than that, since it had been inherited by Francis from her late grandmother, known as Mother Eve.

Francis was accused of having caused illness in people by means of sorcery, two of the people in question being William Auger and Mary Cocke. It was also alleged that she had enlisted the help of her cat Sathan to punish a wealthy man who had refused to marry her, first by ruining him financially and then by killing him. His name was Richard Byles, and he did indeed soon lose first his wealth and then his life.

The enterprising cat then supposedly found Francis another husband, one Christopher Francis, but it appears that all was not well with the marriage. A baby appeared on the scene and this was not part of Elizabeth Francis's plan. Consequently she got Sathan to kill the baby. Christopher Francis apparently was not measuring up to his wife's expectations and again she enlisted the help of her trusty cat. This time he assumed the shape of a toad and hid in the husband's shoe so that he was able to come into contact with the man's foot and so cause lameness. Toads were not to be meddled with in witchcraft lore.

After this, Francis gave the cat to Agnes Waterhouse. The

reason for the gift is not known. It seems strange that such a helpful companion was given away. However, it appears that Sathan continued to play havoc.

In the trials of 1566 Francis was more fortunate than Agnes Waterhouse. She was found guilty but her life was spared and her punishment confined to terms of imprisonment and appearances in the pillory. She was not so fortunate, however, in the Chelmsford trials of 1579. Francis confessed to charges of witchcraft, having previously said that she had been taught the basics of the art at the feet of her late grandmother, known as Mother Eve, the original owner of Sathan (page 181). She was duly judged guilty of witchcraft and hanged along with Ellen Smith (page 183) and Alice Nokes (page 163).

Gerald Gardner

Born near Liverpool in 1884 into a family of Scottish descent, he played an extremely large part in reviving witchcraft in the twentieth century. The family claimed as an ancestor Grizell Gairdner, who had been burnt as a witch at Newburgh in Scotland in 1640, and Gerald Gardner's grandfather had married a woman who was reputed to be a witch.

He worked for a considerable time in the Far East and became interested in the spiritual beliefs of some of the local people. When he retired and returned home to Britain in 1936 he developed his interest in archaeology and became interested in witchcraft. He and his wife lived in the New Forest area and became members of a coven there in 1939. In 1946 Gardner was introduced to Aleister Crowley (page 122).

It was Gardner's wish to write about witchcraft, but at that time witchcraft was still illegal in Britain, the law banning it not being repealed until 1951. He had to content himself with writing about witchcraft in a novel based on witchcraft rituals until the witchcraft ban was lifted and he was able to write *Witchcraft Today*, published in 1954, which presented modern witchcraft as the survivor of an ancient pagan religion. Gardner was much influenced in his theories by the work of Margaret Murray, who put forward the theory that witchcraft was a continuation of a pagan religion in her book *The Witch-cult in Western Europe*, published in 1921 (*see* page 13).

The publication of Gardner's book aroused much interest in witchcraft, and many people wrote to him asking for advice. Numerous covens were set up, some of them scandalising people by gathering in the nude in the open air and performing sexual acts as part of their rituals.

In 1951, the year in which Gardner set up his own coven, he went to the Isle of Man to become manager of a museum of magic and witchcraft, which he extended and later bought. He continued to write on the subject of witchcraft, his works including *The Meaning of Witchcraft*, published in 1959. He also helped to compile a book of witchcraft rituals, known as a book of shadows. This is the name given to a book of beliefs, rituals, spells, etc, which acts as a guide for the practice of witchcraft. There is no definitive work, and each tradition and coven can adapt it for their particular use. Gardner was helped in his compilation of his book of shadows by Doreen Valiente, a member of his coven. The book became known as the standard guide to the Gardnerian tradition of witchcraft.

Shortly before his death he met Raymond Buckland (page 110), with whom he had corresponded and whom he had influenced greatly so that Buckland introduced the Gardnerian tradition of witchcraft to America. Gardner died aboard ship in February 1964 on his way back from a journey to the Lebanon and was buried in Tunis.

Louis Gaufridi

Gaufridi was a priest accused of bewitching nuns in a convent in Aix-en-Provence. The case bears some similarities to the later case of Urbain Grandier (page 140), and it is thought that Gaufridi's case was taken as a kind of precedent for Grandier's. At any rate, both involved a priest, both involved nuns and charges of demonic possession, and both had distinctly sexual elements.

Gaufridi, who came from Marseilles, was, like Grandier, an exceptionally handsome man. He was friendly with a wealthy family named Demandolx, and when he was thirty-four he showed this friendship by trying to help the family's thirteen year-old daughter, Madeleine, who appears to have been suffering from mental problems. He began to spend a great deal of time with the girl and, despite her youth and the age difference between them, rumours being to circulate as to the nature of their relationship.

The priest was advised by his superiors of the rumours and cautioned him to limit his visits. In 1607 the situation appeared to resolve itself when Madeleine went to the Ursuline convent at Marseilles to begin her noviciate. On arrival there, she confessed that she had had a full-blown affair with Gaufridi and she was despatched to a sister convent in Aix-en-Provence to try to prevent any further meetings.

At the end of 1609 Madeleine began to suffer fits and went on to claim to being possessed by demons at the instigation of Father Gaufridi. Attempts were made to exorcise the demons but her fits and allegations continued. Meanwhile Madeleine grew more insistent that she had had a sexual affair with the priest and gave more and more detailed accounts of this. Gaufridi denied any such sexual involvement with her.

It was common in accusations of witchcraft or demoniac possession for people to affect each other, especially if the accusers were young girls or members of a close community. True to form, Madeleine's hysterical outbursts began to be copied by other nuns, of whom Louise Capel was the worst affected.

Madeleine and Louise were ordered to appear before the Grand Inquisitor in Avignon. The two young women gave colourful details of the demons that were meant to possess them. Attempts to exorcise these failed. Gaufridi was then asked to conduct a session of exorcism, a procedure that was to be repeated in the case of Urbaine Grandier.

The process was not successful and the priest was imprisoned. There being little evidence of witchcraft or demoniac possession against him, he was released and appealed to the head of his church, the Pope, to take some action against the girls and their fraudulent claims. Madeleine was ordered to be subjected to supervision, but her hysteria worsened, and her speech and actions became very lewd.

Eventually the case came to trial in 1611. Madeleine's behaviour was, to say the least, unstable. Sometimes she was on the side of Gaufridi, denying her claims and asking him for forgiveness, and sometimes she was on the side of the prosecution, raving about demonic possession and sexual perversions.

Meanwhile Gaufridi had been languishing in jail. Having been inspected for evidence of the devil's mark, a mark, often a mark of insensitivity, supposedly imprinted by the devil on the bodies of those who had sworn allegiance to him, and this almost inevitably having been found since practically any mark could be so categorised, he was formally charged. After severe torture, in sheer desperation, he admitted to the charges, agreeing that he had signed a pact with the devil in order to satisfy his lust for Madeleine and other women.

He later retracted these charges, but he was found guilty and sentenced to death. His body was subjected to terrible torture before execution in order to try to force him to name accomplices but he did not do so. He was strangled and burnt to ashes on the stake.

In 1642, and again in 1652, Madeleine herself was accused of witchcraft. Evidence of the devil's mark was found upon her body and she was imprisoned for life. She died in 1670.

Sarah Good

One of the Salem Witches (page 174), Sarah Good was one of the first to be accused by the girls. She was a poor woman who begged to keep her family alive, her husband being shiftless. Given her circumstances, no one protested much at the accusations against her. Furthermore, Tituba (page 185) claimed that she had travelled through the air with her to coven meetings and that she kept a familiar in the form of a yellow bird. She was found guilty and executed on 19 July 1692 alongside Rebecca Nurse (page 165).

Alice Goodridge

Accused of witchcraft in 1596 on the evidence of Thomas Darling, known as the Burton Boy because he lived in Burton-on-Trent, she faced the charges simply because she had the misfortune to meet the boy in local woods on a day when he later fell ill. People suspected that his illness might have been caused by witchcraft when he began to have fits and to speak of seeing visions of the devil and other demons, especially one in the form of a green cat.

When asked if he had seen anyone in the woods on the day he had been taken ill, Darling racked his brains and remembered that he had had an encounter with an elderly woman. He remembered the incident because she complained when he broke wind in her presence and recited a poem that indicated that because of his action she would go to heaven and he would go to hell. His description of her clothes and of three warts on her face led his relatives to deduce that the person whom he had met was Goodridge, who lived nearby.

Goodridge, whilst readily admitting that she had met the boy in the woods, gave an entirely different version of events. She claimed that he had taunted her with abuse, saying that she was a witch. Her claims were to no avail, as Darling's fits and visions increased in intensity when Goodridge was brought near to him. She was subjected to various tests for witchcraft, and her failure to recite the Lord's Prayer was regarded as proof of her guilt. This supposed proof was underlined by the fact that a local man claimed that she had bewitched his cow. It was extremely common when anyone was accused of witchcraft for others to rush in with tales that made her plight worse.

She was submitted to tortures in order to make her confess, one of these forms of torture including the placing of her feet in shoes and the positioning of her feet so close to a fire that the shoes grew quite unbearably hot. Despite this extreme discomfort and pain, she refused to make a confession but did admit to keeping a dog that had been given to her by her mother. This was taken by the authorities to be a familiar of the kind regularly kept by witches. Because there was a deep suspicion that witchcraft ran in families, especially in the female line, Goodridge's mother, Elizabeth Wright (page 199), was also accused of witchcraft.

Goodridge was duly declared guilty of witchcraft but before the death sentence could be carried out she died in Derby jail. As was often the case with those who brought charges of witchcraft, Darling was later to admit that he had made the whole thing up in order to draw attention to himself.

Isobel Gowdie

A young and attractive self-confessed witch, Gowdie lived in Auldearn in Morayshire in Scotland. She made her confessions in 1662 without any threat of the tortures that were usually used to extract confessions from supposed witches. Quite why she confessed to witchcraft so readily is not known, although various possibilities have been put forward.

The suggestions include that she was mad, that she was desperately bored with her rather uninteresting farmer husband, and consequently with her childless marriage, and craved the excitement and attention that was brought to her by her explicit claims of sexual intercourse with the devil – huge genitals and semen like ice – and her accounts of orgiastic meetings of her coven of thirteen witches. One can deduce something of her relationship with her husband from the fact that, when she was out at one of her coven meetings or enjoying one of her sexual sessions with the devil, her husband was completely convinced that she was in bed beside him, she having had the forethought to substitute a broomstick, a symbol of witchcraft, for her body.

Gowdie also gave detailed descriptions of the activities of the coven to which she belonged. These included transforming themselves into various animals, such as cats and hares; raising storms by beating wet rags frenziedly on stones while reciting spells; making clay models of enemies with a view to bringing about their destruction; ruining farmers' crops by burying the bodies of unchristened children in their manure heaps, the bodies having been specially dug up for the occasion; aiming elf-arrows at people, these magic arrows being designed to cause illness and misfortune in both humans and animals; and making previously fertile land barren by using a miniature plough pulled by toads to dig it up.

All the activities admitted to by Gowdie were those traditionally associated with witchcraft. She further sought to establish her status as a witch by claiming to have the devil's mark an area of the body, in her case the shoulder, from which the devil was said to have sucked blood or otherwise marked his witch followers, often traditionally by raking his claw over them, licking them, burning them with a hot iron, etc, in a symbolic gesture to seal their pledge to be his servants. Although Gowdie gloried in having such a mark, many accused witches had cause to regret the presence of scars or natural blemishes since these were assumed by the authorities to be devil's marks. It was claimed that experts, such as were supposedly used as inspectors in witch trials could differentiate between a birthmark, scar or natural blemish and the mark of the devil but this was far from true. Not many people enjoy unblemished bodies and a surprising number of women accused of witchcraft were found by the experts to have been marked by the devil.

Whatever the reason for Gowdie's remarkable claims, and whatever the state of her sanity at the time, there is no doubt that she was a positive gift to the authorities since she claimed to encompass the whole range of activities associated with witchcraft. She seemed to welcome the punishment that she knew would accompany confessions of witchcraft, remarking that she deserved tortures such as being stretched on an iron rack or having her body torn asunder by wild horses. Perhaps she was also some kind of masochist.

What happened to Gowdie is not indicated by any records, as the trial proceedings are for some reason incomplete. It seems likely, however, that she suffered the fate suffered by others found guilty of witchcraft and was put to death, her body having been burned to ashes. It is likely, also, that those accomplices whom she had named in her confession, as was part of the tradition of witch trials, were also painfully executed.

Urbain Grandier

Appointed parish priest of St-Pierre-du-Marche in Loudun, a town in Poitiers in France, in 1617, Urbain was handsome and fond of women. It was alleged that this fondness for the opposite sex went beyond what it should have done, given his vows of celibacy. He was popularly supposed to have had relationships with several young women and he was suspected of being the father of the child of Philippa Trincant, whose father held an administrative post in the town. In addition, he was assumed to have taken as his mistress Madeleine du Brou, whose father was also part of the town's administration.

In 1630 he was arrested on charges of immorality, tried by

the Bishop of Poitiers and found guilty. Although Urbain had made powerful enemies he also had powerful friends and was reinstated to his post within a year. Urbain so far had survived despite his reputation, but Jeanne des Anges, Mother Superior of the Ursuline Convent, was to be his undoing.

It is not entirely clear whether the hysteria in the nuns, which was identified as demonic possession caused by Grandier, was Jeanne's idea or whether it was suggested to her by Father Mignon, father confessor to the nuns and an enemy of Grandier, being related to Trincant, whose baby Grandier was suspected of fathering. Certainly it was obvious that Mignon wished Grandier harm but it may well have been that Jeanne, who had turned her back on fleshly pleasures, wished to make Grandier pay for his lust and lack of celibacy. The Mother Superior of the convent, formerly Madame de Beclier, before becoming a nun, was of a wealthy family and was supposedly extravagant and even wild in her secular life before settling down to a life of piety.

Whatever the truth behind the plot to bring about the downfall of Grandier, Jeanne began to claim that Grandier was appearing to her in her dreams and was trying to seduce her into sexual acts and other vices. She began to rave and throw fits, and some of the other nuns followed suit. Mignon and his assistant were brought in to exorcise the nuns, and Jeanne claimed that she and some of her fellow nuns were possessed by two demons, Asmodeus and Zabulon, whom she claimed had been conjured up by Grandier sent to her in a bouquet of roses that had been thrown over the convent wall.

News of the nuns' condition and supposed demonic possession spread through the town, and Grandier could see that things were not looking too good for him. In an effort to counteract the damage being done to him by the nuns' ravings, he approached his friend the Archbishop of Bordeaux for help. The archbishop ordered the nuns to be examined by his doctor who found no evidence of possession and declared the nuns to be fakes. At this the archbishop ordered Mignon's exorcism to be brought to an end and the nuns to be confined in their cells.

This appeared to have ended the nuns' hysteria and hallucinations, and for a while all was quiet. The peace was to be short-lived, however, and hysteria broke out again later that year.

Grandier had made powerful enemies in the course of his life, among these no less a person than Cardinal Richelieu. He was supposedly the author of a satire against Richelieu in 1618, and this had been brought to the Cardinal's attention. Unfortunately for Grandier, one of Richelieu's relatives was one of the Loudun nuns, and he was not best pleased to hear that the nuns had been accused of faking demonic possession.

Richelieu, in an effort to get his revenge on Grandier, appointed Jean de Laubardemont head of a commission to investigate the nuns' claims. The exorcisms were resumed, and this time they were held in public. The nuns responded with fits, ravings, a series of obscene postures and descriptions of hallucinations. Members of the public found all this very shocking, particularly because the women were in holy orders. Grandier's position was looking rather desperate and, to make matters worse, some of his former mistresses came forward with stories of Grandier's adultery and fornication, conducted in the church itself and therefore sacrilegious.

Finally Grandier himself was ordered to officiate at one of the public exorcisms. The nuns' behaviour grew more wild and their claims more extravagant. Grandier was accused of witchcraft and put in prison in the castle of Angiers in 1633. He was duly searched for evidence of the devil's mark (page 254). Such a mark was allegedly found on Grandier's body, although it was claimed that the reason why certain areas on his body seemed insensitive to pain or touch was that he had been cut or stabbed so severely elsewhere that his attention was so focused on the pain of the wound that he failed to notice being touched elsewhere. The physician who was in charge of preparing Grandier for torture denied the presence on his body of devil's marks, as did the Poitiers apothecary, but they were ignored.

The supposed presence of devil's marks simply added to the danger of Grandier's situation. He was already in a great deal of trouble, and this had been added to by the production of a piece of paper that was alleged to be a pact between Grandier and the devil, signed in blood by Grandier and countersigned by the devil and various demons. It was claimed that this piece of evidence had been taken from the devil's own files by the demon Asmodeus, one of those who had supposedly possessed the nuns.

This was clearly an extremely unlikely story, but it was accepted as evidence of Grandier's involvement with the devil and with witchcraft. The allegation was so bizarre that it had the effect of making some people think that things had gone quite far enough. Voices were raised in Grandier's defence and even some of the nuns spoke in his favour, offering to make a retraction of their allegations against him.

Given Richelieu's determination to bring about the downfall, and preferably death, of Grandier, it was clearly unwise to speak in the latter's defence. People wishing to give evidence for the defence were encouraged to remain silent lest they themselves be charged with witchcraft. As for the nuns' suggested retraction, it was treated by the prosecution as evidence that the devil was helping his servant Grandier. Even the sight of Jeanne d'Anges in court with a noose around her neck, threatening to hang herself if she were not allowed to retract the allegations of demonic possession that had brought Grandier to his present perilous situation, was to no avail. It is said that some of the nuns were offered pensions by Richelieu if they would agree to appear for the prosecution.

Grandier was duly found guilty in August 1634 and sentenced to death by hanging and then burning at the stake. Throughout the trial and post-trial proceedings, Grandier steadfastly declared his innocence of any crimes connected with witchcraft or the devil. Unlike many people accused of witchcraft, the priest refused to implicate anyone else. This refusal to suggest that he had accomplices in his alleged witchcraft further angered his accusers, and extreme torture was used in order to make him do so. They broke both his legs in such a horrible manner that it was said that marrow was seen to ooze from his broken limbs. When he prayed to God for help, they said that he was invoking the aid of his master, the devil.

Still he refused to implicate others, and his tormentors took their final revenge. He was supposed to be allowed to make a last statement before hanging, but when he began to declaim his innocence, the friars who were supervising his execution threw so much holy water on his head that he was prevented from speaking. Furthermore, he had been sentenced to be hanged before being burned, as was usually the case, but in order to subject him to as much agony as possible, the noose was so tied that it could not be tightened. Thus the rope did not strangle him and when he went to the stake he was still alive.

It was to be expected that the death of Grandier would see the end of the nuns' hysterical antics, supposedly caused by demonic possession instigated by him. However, this was not the case. The antics continued and were even more lewd than before. The language of the nuns caught up in these hysterical outbursts grew more and more crude. People were shocked to hear of this, but this did not prevent them from rushing to witness the public exorcisms for themselves to see and hear the goings-on.

Eventually, in 1637, the niece of Cardinal Richelieu, the Duchess d'Aiguillon, protested to her uncle about the lewd show the nuns were putting on. By this time he had no interest in the affair, having demonstrated his power and having got rid of a priest who might have caused him political problems, and Richelieu simply stopped paying the money to the nuns that had been awarded to them during the trial. This had the effect of dramatically lessening the activity of the nuns.

Jeanne d'Anges continued to have hysterical fits and was not seemingly cured of these until a visit to Italy to seek help from the tomb of St Francis de Sales in 1638. She died in 1665. Her role in the accusations made against Grandier are subject to debate. Some say that she was a complete fraud, wishing to harm Grandier, some say that she was an attention-seeker, some say that she probably suffered from epilepsy and others that she may have suffered from schizophrenia. Whatever the truth of the matter, she certainly succeed in drawing attention to herself and to the town of Loudun.

The history of all this was the subject of a book by Aldous Huxley, *The Devils of Loudun* (1952), and the subject of a Ken Russell film, *The Devils* (1971).

Dorothy Green

One of the Morpeth Witches, Green was accused with Mary Hunter of casting a spell over a mare belonging to a local man, John March, the spell resulting in the animal's death. March, himself, claimed that a swallow would not leave the horse alone one evening and after this harassment the mare had become ill. Four days later it was dead. Thus did people come to connect any misfortune with witchcraft.

The Morpeth trial records are not very helpful, but it seems likely that the accused witches, including Green, all of whom pleaded not guilty, were acquitted.

Rebecca Greensmith

One of the Connecticut Witches (page 117), Greensmith was accused of witchcraft in the town of Hartford in 1662 on the evidence of a girl called Ann Cole. Cole became subject to fits, and this was construed to be a result of possession by the devil or demons. In the course of these fits she is said to have made accusations in Dutch, a language that she did not speak, against a Dutch girl living locally and against Greensmith.

The Dutch girl was fortunate enough to be acquitted but Greensmith was not so lucky. When Cole made her accusations Greensmith was already being held on other charges of witchcraft. The claim that was the basis of the latter charges was that she had been seen in the company of strangely dressed demons, although it was later suggested that these might have been North American Indians wearing ceremonial headdresses.

Greensmith did her case untold harm by claiming to have had intercourse with the devil after he had appeared before her in the form of a deer. With this evidence from her own lips she could hope for nothing other than a charge of guilty and the death sentence. Her husband, Nathaniel, was also convicted and put to death with her, although he denied knowing anything about her involvement with witchcraft and protested his own innocence.

Nathaniel was not the only one to go to his death on the evidence of Greensmith. It was her contention that a coven of witches was in the habit of gathering at a spot near her house, their members regularly indulging in shape-changing and turning themselves into crows and other creatures. It is likely, as was often the case of people accused or found guilty of witchcraft, that Cole named names and informed the authorities of the identity of the people whom she had seen at the coven. Whether this was the case or not, several others, both men and women, were accused of attending the coven mentioned by Greensmith. They were arrested, tried and at least some them were executed by hanging

Isobel Grierson

Grierson was found guilty of witchcraft and first strangled and then burnt at the stake on the hill of Edinburgh Castle in 1607. She was one of many convicted witches who owed her plight to her neighbours. The wife of a labourer from

Prestonpans, near Edinburgh, Grierson was much disliked and feared by those around her.

Eventually the general animosity against her resulted in one of her neighbours, Adam Clark, accusing her of harming him by means of witchcraft over a period of months. She was supposed, among other activities, to have taken the form of a cat, traditionally a favourite disguise of witches, in order to find a way of getting to the Clark cottage after dark. When there, it was alleged that she and other cats terrified the inhabitants.

As was frequently the way with charges of witchcraft, one charge led to another and other neighbours came up with allegations, glad to see harm come to someone whom they disliked so much. She was accused of making Robert Peddan sick until he eventually paid up some money that he owed her, that she had brought sickness on his wife on several occasions and that she had caused the ale that he was brewing to go bad.

Other neighbours went forward with similar allegations, and Grierson was charged. She was not allowed any defence, a situation that was by no means uncommon, although in fact a defence rarely did any good. As indicated above, she was burned at the stake, the victim of her neighbours' dislike and vengeance.

Louis van Haecke

Haecke (1828–1912) was a Belgian Catholic priest who substituted for the traditional Catholic mass a distorted version at the heart of which was a sexual theme and which included various traditional pagan rites and elements. At these masses, conducted not only in Bruges in Belgium but in Paris also, the priest officiated wearing a skullcap with horns on top of it.

Rites included the desecration of the Christian host, and the orgiastic activities that took place were reminiscent of those claimed to take place at the traditional witches' sabbats.

The priest's obsession with sex and devil-worshipping was brought to light by a writer called Joris-Karl Huysmans. Having heard rumours of the priest's black magic activities, Huysmans persuaded a woman of his acquaintance, named Berthe Courriere, to become part of a coven based in Bruges and to supply him with details as to what took place. When she reported back to him he wrote a novel based on her account, and this came to the ears of the Bishop of Bruges.

The bishop initiated an inquiry into Haecke's alleged activities but the time of witch hysteria had long gone, the inquiry was not pursued with much rigour and was finally dropped.

George Hahn

The Vice-Chancellor of Bamberg at the time when there was mass torture and slaughter of people accused of being Bamberg Witches (page 97), Hahn was so horrified by the situation that he felt compelled to protest. This was a brave thing to do, given the stringent witch-hunts that were going on, and it proved to be foolhardy too. He himself was accused of witchcraft, as were his wife and daughter, and all three were executed in 1628.

The tortures that were in force during the Bamberg Witchcraft Trials (*see* Chapter 2, Witchcraft Trials, page 30) were notorious even by the usual horrific standards of witchcraft trials. As was the case with so many others, Hahn was subjected to such terrible pain that he would have confessed to anything to be free of it. He duly made a formal confession, and, again as was the case with so many others, in the course of his confession made accusations of witchcraft against others. As a result of this five burgomasters were accused and found guilty.

Isobel Haldane

Accused of being a witch, Haldane was tried in Perth in Scotland in 1623. Details of her trial are unusually well documented, and the evidence given against her largely took the form of reports that she had succeeded in curing sick people. It was claimed by her accusers that these powers of healing must have been granted to her by the devil, but Haldane, while admitting to such powers, said that she had learned the art of healing from the fairies. Various people testified to having been helped by her. Some claimed to have received herbal remedies from her and others claimed that she had saved their sick children's lives by the simple expedient of washing them, the theory being that the disease was transferred from the children to the water.

The other major charge against her was that she had the gift of prophesy and had prophesied the death of various local people, these deaths all having occurred in the way that she had foreseen. She accounted for this gift by describing an extremely unusual incident that had befallen her some ten years before.

According to Haldane, she had been lying in bed when she suddenly found herself being taken from the bed by some unidentified force and left on a hillside. The hillside opened and she entered into the opening, staying inside the hill for three days. At the end of these three days she was taken back to the outside world by a man with a grey beard who told her the names of those who were going to die in the near future.

Although there is much detail in the records of Haldane's interrogation, the documentation as to what her fate was is absent. It is likely, however, that in the spirit of the times she suffered a similar fate to those accused of witchcraft, some of them on much shakier evidence, and was found guilty, strangled and burnt at the stake.

Katherine Harrison

One of the Connecticut Witches (page 117), Harrison was fortunate enough to be tried after the first wave of witchcraft hysteria in Connecticut had passed, there being fewer trials after 1662. Although she was tried in 1669 and sentenced to death, these were slightly more clement times and the death sentence was changed to one of banishment.

Catherine Henot

One of the Cologne Witches (page 116), Henot was accused of putting a spell on some of the nuns of the order of St Clare. She was tried by the church court, but Cologne was noted as a city of tolerance and she received a much fairer trial than she would have done elsewhere in Germany. In particular she was allowed her own defence counsel.

The church court, having listened to the evidence, found her not guilty. Alas for Henot, a higher ecclesiastical power in the form of Archbishop Ferdinand of Cologne stepped in and ordered Henot to be tried by a different court. This time it was quite a different story. The second court brought in a verdict of guilty and she was sentenced to death by burning.

Mary Hunter

One of the Morpeth Witches, *see* Dorothy GREEN, page 146.

Isobel Insh

Named by John Stewart (page 185) as one of the accomplices of Margaret Barclay (page 98), Insh was arrested by the authorities who also claimed to have received evidence of her witchcraft from her eight-year-old daughter. She was confined in the belfry tower of the local church and, knowing what tortures lay ahead for an accused witch, tried to escape, from the tower. In so doing she suffered a severe fall and died from her injuries.

Mary Johnson

A native of Wethersfield, Johnson was one of the Connecticut Witches (page 117). Although there was no other evidence, she was tried and hanged after confessing to having been guilty of child murder and to having had sexual intercourse with the devil.

Ursula Kempe

The woman at the heart of the trial concerning the St Osyth Witches, Kempe was a midwife and nursemaid who was also known for her healing skills and allegedly for her skill in undoing spells placed on people by means of sorcery. She was alleged to have successfully cured the illness of a young boy and to have taken offence when the boy's mother, Grace Thurlowe, did not invite her to be nursemaid to her infant daughter. When the child fell out of her cot and broke her neck, there were rumours that Kempe was behind the incident, she having used her magic skills to bring about the death.

No explicit accusations were made and Thurlowe must

have decided to ignore the rumours because she asked Kempe to treat her for an arthritic condition. After prescribing a complicated and bizarre remedy that seemed to help the condition, Kempe was enraged to find that her patient refused to pay her fee.

At this point Thurlowe's complaint began to get worse and she, remembering the previous rumours, began to suspect witchcraft. She therefore made a formal complaint to the authorities and they decided to investigate the matter. Kempe was sent for trial and her eight-year-old son, Thomas Rabbett, was called upon to give evidence against his mother and her witchlike activities. This he did, and it was then suggested to Kempe that she would be treated with leniency by the courts if she made a formal confession of guilt with regard to witchcraft.

Kempe then poured out a confession confirming her son's claim and going into detail about her four familiars, two cats, a toad and a white lamb, and of how she had fed them partly on drops of blood from her body. According to her testimony, the familiars had helped her to commit several crimes. In particular, she alleged that the lamb, unusual as a familiar since traditionally familiars were unable to take the shape of lambs, had rocked the crib in which the Thurlowe child had lain and knocked her out of the crib.

She then put herself at the mercy of the court but not before she had given the names of other women in St Osyth whom she claimed were witches. She claimed to have seen evidence of their activities by peering through their windows and to have received information about their deeds from the white lamb that was her familiar. Neither her confession nor her identification of other supposed witches did her any good.

The prosecution went back on its promise to show clemency if she confessed and she was hanged, after admitting to the causing of three killings by sorcery.

Her allegations against others resulted in a considerable number of people being tried since the people accused by her made accusations against others. Fourteen women were formally charged and two of them, including Kempe, were hanged. The other was Elizabeth Bennet (page 101).

Beatrice Laing

The woman at the centre of the Pittenweem Witches, Laing was accused of witchcraft in 1704 by a young blacksmith's apprentice, Patrick Morton in the village of Pittenweem in Fife in Scotland. He claimed that she took revenge on him for being unable to find the time to forge some nails for her because he was busy with other work. He further claimed that her revenge had taken the form of using magic to make him ill, the illness taking the form of a weakness in the limbs and a tendency to fits. He added to his claims the fact that he had been pinched by Laing and an accomplice and had the marks to prove it.

The local minister backed Morton's claims and Laing was duly tried. After being subjected to some of the tortures that were used on supposed witches to encourage them to confess, principally being forced to stay awake for five days and nights, she made a confession. Not only did she implicate herself, but she named others as her accomplices. One of these, Mrs Nicholas Lawson (page 155), had also been accused by Patrick Morton of aiding and abetting Laing but Janet Cornfoot (page 119) and Isobel Adam (page 94) were now also named.

Laing was among the more fortunate of those who were accused of witchcraft. As was quite common among people who had confessed to witchcraft under the duress of torture, she withdrew her confession after she had recovered sufficiently from the ravages of the torture. She was not executed but placed in the stocks as a warning to others and then thrown into a dungeon to endure solitary confinement for some months.

This may not seem like very benign treatment, although at least she had escaped with her life, but she was eventually released on payment of a small fine. Her suffering did not end there, because her supposed connection with witchcraft meant that her family did not want her at home with them. She had no choice but to become a wanderer and eventually died in St Andrews.

As was frequently the case with charges of witchcraft, the original accuser was found to be a deceiver. Patrick Morton was found to be an impostor, having been encouraged in his accusations by the local minister, Patrick Cowper.

Mrs Nicholas Lawson

One of the so-called Pittenweem Witches, Lawson was accused with Beatrice Laing (page 154) of making a local apprentice blacksmith ill by means of witchcraft because he, Patrick Morton, had refused to carry out work for her. She was further accused by Laing after the latter had been tortured into confessing.

Eliphas Levi

This was the pseudonym of Alphonse Louis Constant, born in 1810 in Paris, who achieved fame as an occultist. Although he developed an interest in magic at quite a young age, he decided to make the church his career and became a priest. This did not prove to be a wise decision as he had great difficulty in observing the vow of chastity and his interest in left-wing politics did not endear him to his superiors. He was jailed for his political writings and dismissed from the church.

Alphonse became more and more interested in the occult and was influenced by a man named Ganneau who claimed to be a reincarnation of Louis XVII and also claimed to have prophetic powers. Renaming himself Eliphas Levi, the Hebrew equivalent of his first and middle names, he took a trip to London in 1854 where he developed his interest in necromancy.

Levi practised magic but he appears to have been more a commentator than a skilled practitioner. He gave lessons in the occult and is best known for his influence on later generations through the medium of his writings, such as *The Dogma and Ritual of High Magic*, in which he wrote extensively about tarot cards, published in 1861, and *A History of Magic*. He had several admirers, among whom was Edward Bulwer-Lytton, an English author whom he visited in England in 1863. The latter was also greatly interested in the occult and appears to have been greatly influenced by Levi. Levi, himself, acknowledged the influence of the English occultist, Francis Barrett (page 99), author of *Magus*, published in 1801.

Temperance Lloyd

One of the Exeter Witches (page 127), Lloyd was held to be queen of the covens to which her co-accused, Susanna Edwards (page 126) and Mary Trembles (page 187), were also supposed to belong. She had already been tried on charges of witchcraft twice before the trial that led to her execution in August 1682 and, like her co-accused, openly admitted to being associated with witchcraft. Like the other two involved in the trial, she was elderly and practically destitute. She is reported to have seemed untroubled by the fact that she was found guilty and is said to have chewed nonchalantly on a piece of bread as she went to the gallows.

Effie Maclean

Properly called Euphemia Maclean, she was one of the people accused of being part of the coven known as the North Berwick Witches (page 163). A feature of the trials concerned with this group was that several of the accused were of high social standing, this being thought to be partly the reason that the king, James I of Scotland, decided to take on the role of interrogator at the trials. Like Barbara Napier (page 163), Maclean was one such person, being the daughter of Cliftonhall.

Unfortunately, neither her highborn connections nor the six lawyers whom she engaged to plead her case were instrumental in saving her life. Her links with the Earl of Bothwell were her undoing because he was rumoured to have initiated plots to kill the king in order to take his place on the throne and so he was the king's sworn enemy.

This attitude of the king influenced his feelings towards any friend or relative of Bothwell and he was determined to show Maclean no mercy despite her position in society, and she was found guilty and executed. It was common for people to be strangled before being burnt at the stake to save then the agony of being burned alive. This privilege was not accorded to Maclean and she went to the stake alive.

Magee Island Witches

The last witch trial to take place in Ireland, in 1711, concerned eight women from Magee Island near Carrickfergus in County Antrim. Tried in Carrickfergus, they were accused by a servant girl, Mary Dunbar. A servant in the house of James Haldridge, she claimed to be being tormented by the spirits of the women and was attacked by seizures or went into fits if she were near any of them. During the seizures she claimed to have vomited up a weird selection of objects, such as feathers, pins and large waistcoat buttons.

The case was further complicated by the fact that shortly before the arrival of Dunbar in Haldane's house, the household had been subjected to what appeared to be poltergeist activity and then Haldridge's mother was stricken with a pain in her back and died a few days later. Witchcraft was suspected and so it was already in the air before Mary Dunbar came on the scene with her accusations.

Seven of the women were arrested, and the women were tried solely on Dunbar's evidence and without a defence counsel. There was a lack of unanimity among the three judges, and there was sympathy for the women because they had been previously believed to be of good character and were regular attenders at church. However, the jury found them guilty. Compared with many of the sentences for witchcraft theirs were relatively light. They were not executed but subjected to a year each in prison and also had to undergo four periods each in the pillory.

Andrew Mann

By his own confession a witch, Mann, in order to save himself from trial and execution, and doubtless to obtain financial gain, as was the case with most witch-finders, turned king's evidence and was appointed by the authorities as an official witch-finder, his task involving the naming of witches and providing the initial evidence to enable the authorities to embark on the trial.

Magdalen Mattsdotter

One of the witches involved in the Mora Witch Trials in Sweden, she was accused of witchcraft by her own children and her servant girls. She was burnt at the stake but it was later found that the servant girls had invented the whole charge out of envy of their mistress. It was by no means unusual in the general hysteria that surrounded witch trials for servants to trump up charges against their mistresses.

One of the main features of these Swedish witch trials was the number of children involved. Indeed, it was children who first brought the allegations of witchcraft in the area to light. Some of these were executed along with many adults and even more were severely punished in other ways.

Alice Molland

Generally held to be the last person to be officially executed in England for supposedly practising witchcraft, her hanging taking place in Exeter in 1684. It has been suggested that two women were hanged in Northampton as late as 1705 and that, even later, in 1716, a woman and child were hanged in

Huntingdon. Because of a lack of records these claims are thought to be fictitious.

Although Molland may have been the last person to be officially hanged for supposed connections with witchcraft, she was not the last to die because of charges of witchcraft. Many died when they were set about by mobs of people who were convinced they were witches and many also died in the course of being subjected to the cruel tests that were used in an attempt to establish that someone was a witch.

Nanny Morgan

Although she lived a considerable time after supposed witches had ceased to be prosecuted, Nanny Morgan (1789–1857), who lived near Much Wenlock in Shropshire, was suspected by many people in the area of being involved in witchcraft. The end of witchcraft as a legal offence did not destroy belief in witchcraft and such belief was often stronger in rural areas.

Her reputation as a witch was based partly on the fact that she told fortunes, an art she was supposed to have learnt from a gang of gypsies with whom she travelled around in her youth. It was also based on the fact that she was alleged to keep live toads in her cottage and toads were much connected with witchcraft, often supposedly acting as witches' familiars.

Some of her neighbours were convinced that Morgan had the power of the evil eye, this meaning that she could do them harm in some way simply by fixing them with a stare. Many of them were thus extremely nervous of her and would go to great lengths not to offend her.

This was manifested by the attitude of her lodger, William Davis, to her. It was his wish to give up his lodgings in her cottage and to live elsewhere but he was scared to tell her of his intended departure in case she became angry and practised her magic on him. Some of her neighbours advised him that if his landlady did indeed put some kind of spell on him he could undo the influence of this by using a technique known as scoring above the breath. This involved drawing blood from an accused witch from an area above their mouth and nose.

Shortly after this advice was given, Davis left Morgan's house. It was noticed that his clothing was stained with blood and when Morgan was found dead, killed by a series of stab wounds, Davis was immediately suspected of murder. He confessed that he had indeed committed the crime but had done so only in an attempt draw blood and to undo the effects of any spells that she had put on him.

Morpeth Witches *see* Anne FORSTER.

Maria Renata Singer von Mosau

One of the last people to be at the centre of an episode of witchcraft hysteria in Germany, which saw so many witch trials, she was put to death in 1749. She was a nun in a convent near Würzburg and had been well respected for many years when she felt moved to challenge in 1745 the acceptance of one Cecilia Pistorini to the convent. The latter suffered from seizures and hallucinations and Mosau considered that she was not a suitable candidate for the order.

Her objections were set aside and Pistorini was duly admitted to the order. Shortly after this, some of the other nuns began suffering from seizures and showing other signs popularly held to be associated with demonic possession. One of these nuns died and accused Mosau of having been the instigator of her possession by demons.

An investigation was begun, and Oswald Loschert, the Abbot of Oberzell, was disposed to believe the allegations of witchcraft against Mosau. Services of exorcism were conducted with a view to ridding the nuns of their seizures and demons, but no improvement was perceived. Meanwhile Mosau was confined to her cell. When a search was made of the cell, various herbs and potions are alleged to have been uncovered. On the basis of this and other evidence, the nun was charged and subjected to torture.

In the course of torture she made a formal confession of guilt and claimed that she had been introduced to witchcraft in Vienna by a grenadier who had then introduced her to the devil in Prague. After this meeting she turned from her faith in God and made a pact with the devil when she was a child of fourteen. According to her testimony, she had been following the devil's instructions when she had entered the convent at the age of nineteen and had thereafter received regular visits from him in her cell. She confessed also to flying on a broomstick to witches' gatherings in Würzburg. She did not implicate other people in her confessions, a common practice in witchcraft trials when hysteria surrounding sorcery was at its height.

As well as admitting to causing demonic possession in her fellow nuns, Mosau confessed to desecrating the host, clearly a terrible crime in the eyes of the church. In order to prove how she had succeeded in stealing the host, she showed to the authorities the scars of the wound that she had made in her body to conceal the host. Mosau was charged with, and found guilty of, witchcraft and heresy.

She was beheaded in Mareinberg in June 1749 and her corpse burned to ashes.

Barbara Napier

One of the people accused of being part of a coven known as the North Berwick Witches (page 163), Napier put in a plea that she was pregnant when she was called to trial and was given special dispensation and allowed to go free. An unusual feature of the trials relating to the North Berwick Witches was that some of the accused were of high birth or had aristocratic connections, this being one of the factors said to have encouraged King James I to take on the role of interrogator. Napier was such a person, being related to the Laird of Carschoggill.

Alice Nokes

Nokes was one of the Chelmsford Witches (page 111) who was tried in the second wave of witchcraft trials to hit Chelmsford. She was tried at the same time as Elizabeth Francis (page 130), the charge being that she had caused death by means of sorcery. She confessed to being a witch and was executed by hanging.

North Berwick Witches

This refers to an alleged coven of witches operating in the region of East Lothian near Edinburgh. The methods of torture used in their trial (1590–92) were most severe, and indeed the hysteria surrounding this trial was to spread throughout Scotland and England, leading to other horrific trials.

The trials were particularly noteworthy in that they involved the king, King James VI of Scotland, later James I of England. Some of the accused claimed that they had plotted together with the help of the devil to raise a storm to sink the ship in which he sailed to Denmark to collect the woman who was to be his wife. Later confessions included suggestions that members of the coven had made a wax model of the king and melted it, preparing some kind of magic powder made from parts of a corpse and a shroud. Another confession claimed that the coven had tried unsuccessfully to get hold of an article of clothing from the royal wardrobe with a view to smearing this with poison procured from the body of a black toad that had been suspended by its feet for three days.

The king decided to officiate at some of the trials himself, and thus began his interest in witchcraft, which was to lead him to write a treatise on witchcraft, entitled *Daemonologie*, published five years after the end of the trial. There was much public interest in the trial, partly because of the involvement of the king, partly because of the high social standing of some of the accused and partly because of the sensational nature of the detail of some of the confessions.

The coven identified as the North Berwick Witches included Gilly Duncan (page 125), the first to be accused. On giving her confession after extremely painful torture, as was often the case with people accused of witchcraft, she claimed a list of people as being her accomplices. These included Agnes Sampson (page 175), whose trial was noted for the sensational detail covered by her confession forced out of her by terrible tortures. Some of these revelations involved the king. The revelations grew more and more sensational so as to be completely unbelievable but the king angrily insisted that he believed them.

Other supposed members of the coven were Barbara Napier (page 163) and Effie Maclean (page 157), who were both of high social standing. John Fian (page 127), a school-teacher, was also accused of being involved. All of these had had the finger of suspicion pointed at them by Gilly Duncan, and Sampson, Maclean and Fian were all found guilty and put to death.

Rebecca Nurse

One of the Salem Witches (page 174), she was an extremely pious person and one of the most respected people in the community. Consequently many people were shocked by the girls' claims about her. It is widely believed that if the girls had begun their accusations with someone such as Rebecca Nurse the Salem situation would not have got as out of hand as it did because people would have viewed the girls' accusations with incredulity. Unfortunately, by the time Nurse was accused the situation had already gone too far, with most people all too ready to believe the girls' hysterical claims.

At the time of the accusations she was an invalid and aged seventy-one. Originally accused of having her spectre beat Ann Putnam and of having had her spectre try to get Mrs Thomas Putnam, Ann's mother, to sign a devil's pact, she then was accused of having brought about the painful death of Benjamin Holton after an argument over his pigs getting into her fields. Despite her upstanding reputation, her age and her frailty, she was found guilty and hanged on 19 July 1692.

Isobel Ogg

One of the supposed witches in the Aberdeen witch trials in 1596, she was accused of raising storms. This was a common accusation directed at those against whom evidence of witchcraft was being sought, the charge being that they were conspiring with the devil to bring on such storms. *See* Chapter 2, Witchcraft Trials, page 69.

Margaret Ogg

One of the supposed witches involved in the witchcraft trials in Aberdeen in 1596, she was accused of poisoning meat. *See* Aberdeen Witches, page 93.

Sarah Osborne

One of the Salem Witches (page 174), she was an easy target for the girls, being old and bedridden. Furthermore, she had been involved in local scandal, having had her servant staying in her house with her before she married him, and had been married several times. Local people did not feel moved to protest when she was accused. Tituba (page 185) claimed that she had travelled through the air with her to coven meetings and that she kept a familiar in the shape of a winged creature with a woman's head. She died in prison.

Mary Parsons

One of the Connecticut Witches (page 117), she confessed to various witchcraft activities in the town of Springfield, Massachusetts. In 1651 she was tried in Boston for the murder of her child. Although found guilty, she was later reprieved.

Pendle Witches

A coven of witches who were alleged to indulge in witchcraft in the Pendle Forest in Lancashire, the Pendle Witches were at the centre of a mass trial in 1612. The trial, which became known as one of the most notorious in England, would perhaps never have come to be if it had not been for the fierce rivalry of two local peasant families.

The two women considered to be at the head of these families were once close friends and had long been rumoured locally to dabble in witchcraft, being at the very least exponents of herbal remedies. One was Elizabeth Sowthern, known as Old Demdike, and the other was Anne Whittle, known as Old Chattox. Both women had two of the major requisites of one likely to be accused of witchcraft. They were both elderly women and they were both extremely physically unattractive, being archetypal withered hags. People were said to be scared of the very sight of them

The friendship of the two women, and consequently of that of their families, came to an abrupt end in 1601. As with many family feuds throughout history, the feud was based on a seemingly petty incident. It was begun by the granddaughter of Sowthern, Alison Device, reporting the theft of clothes linen and some meal. The following Sunday Alison claimed that she saw some of the missing items being worn by Anne Redfearne, daughter of Whittle. This was enough to set in train a series of accusations and counter-accusations that was to result in a bitter feud.

It was popularly supposed that Whittle was the more powerful of the two old crones as far as witchcraft was concerned, and Alison's father, John Device, was afraid that she would use her expertise in the black art to bring harm to his family. He thus decided to try to prevent this by promising to give Whittle an annual gift of meal in order to appease her wrath. This appears to have worked well enough as a pacifier until John's death.

Thereafter the feud started up again and was vicious enough to come to the attention of a local justice of the peace, Roger Nowell. He set about the well-nigh impossible task of investigating and of putting an end to the incessant quarrelling between the families. Once again there was a series of accusations and counter-accusations as both families sought to outdo each other in extravagant claims of wrongdoing. This proved to be their great disadvantage because claims of witchcraft emerged.

It was said that Sowthern had turned to witchcraft many years before and had sold her soul to the devil in return for him arranging for her to have anything she wanted. From then on, allegedly, the devil visited her in various forms on several occasions. Whittle, not to be outdone, was also said to have sold her soul. Various members of both families were also said to have been converted to witchcraft.

Nowell, the justice of the peace, hearing some of this, became alarmed and decided to investigate the allegations of witchcraft. Accordingly, he imprisoned in Lancaster Castle three of the women who had been allegedly associated with the black art. These were Elizabeth Sowthern, Anne Whittle and Whittle's married daughter, Anne Redfearne.

As they awaited trial they were joined in their jail by Sowthern's granddaughter, Alison Device, then aged eleven, the girl who had started the family feud by making accusations of theft. She was imprisoned on charges of having bewitched a pedlar who had refused to give her some pins, after which he became ill with pains in his side.

Alison admitted to cursing the man and to being of the opinion that she had caused his illness by doing so. Meanwhile Sowthern openly admitted to being a witch. By the time they were brought to trial they had been joined by others accused of witchcraft and many of these were from the two feuding families. More were to join them after it was reported that members of the feuding families had got together to plot to blow up Lancaster Castle in order to release the prisoners from it.

By this time there was a goodly number of people awaiting trial, the accused being charged with the deeds generally associated with witchcraft, such as causing harm to livestock, but also being charged with several killings. At the trial the son and daughter of one of the accused, Elizabeth Device, both gave evidence against her, with sensational accusations of her involvement with witchcraft. The son was simpleminded and the daughter was well under the minimum age for witnesses of fourteen, but these facts were not taken into consideration. Their mother made a full confession of witchcraft.

At the end of the trial, ten of the accused were sentenced to be hanged. Sowthern had been spared the gallows by dying in prison before the beginning of the trial but her former friend and enemy, Whittle, was hanged, as was Anne Redfearne, Whittle's daughter, Alison Device, Sowthern's granddaughter, and Elizabeth Device, among others. Partly because of the sheer numbers involved the trial became known throughout the north of England.

Joan Petersen

Known as the Wapping Witch, Petersen appears to have used such as powers as she had for the good of her fellow men, so, if she were a witch at all, was likely to have been a white witch. Because she had been helpful to many, in that she had seemed to cure illness in people and livestock, there appears to have been several people who wished to come forward to speak in her defence when she was accused of witchcraft. It is said that of these some were frightened into not testifying, doubtless being afraid that they in turn might be accused of witchcraft, and others were bribed not to give supportive evidence.

Although her supporters were discouraged from attending the trial, there were people who were hostile to her who were all too eager to attend. They accused her of some of the charges usual in witchcraft trials – that she had cast spells on people, in particular on a child, and that she had a familiar, a squirrel rather than the more usual cat or dog.

One of the judges at Petersen's trial, Sir John Danvers, a friend of Oliver Cromwell, seemed unduly set on finding her guilty. The reasons for this are unclear but the result was in no doubt. Petersen was found guilty and hanged at Tyburn in 1652.

Pittenweem Witches

A set of supposed witches located in the fishing village of Pittenweem in Fife in Scotland in the early eighteenth century. The charges of witchcraft were set in train by the allegations of an apprentice blacksmith, Patrick Morton. He accused two women, Beatrice Laing (page 154) and later Mrs Nicholas Lawson (page 155), of damaging his health by means of witchcraft because he had been too busy to forge some nails for Laing. Morton was later found to have made the whole thing up, possibly because of the ant-witchcraft teachings of the local minister, Patrick Cowper, but not before Laing had been tortured into confessing and had implicated Janet Cornfoot (page 119) and Isobel Adam (page 94) and others. *See* Pittenweem Witchcraft Trial, page 40.

Elizabeth Proctor

One of the Salem Witches (page 174), Elizabeth Proctor was the wife of John Proctor (page 171). They were the employers of one of the girls involved in the hysterical accusations, Mary Warren. The latter at one point tried to retract her accusations once the Proctors had been arrested but the other girls refused to allow this and accused her of being a witch so that she had to reaffirm the charges and say that the spectre of John Proctor had tormented and made her sign the devil's pact. Both Elizabeth and John Proctor were regarded as being upstanding citizens, but by the time they were charged the hysteria was such that no one was safe from being charged and convicted. Elizabeth Proctor was found guilty but was not executed because she was pregnant. Later she was reprieved.

John Proctor

One of the Salem Witches (page 174), husband of Elizabeth Proctor (page 171). Both of them, particularly John, annoyed the authorities by their condemnation of the proceedings and their refusal to believe in witchcraft. Mary Warren, one of the girls involved in the hysterical charges of witchcraft, was the servant of the Proctors, and when she first began having her fits, John threatened to beat her. The fits disappeared, only to come back after the threat was over. Warren bore her employers, particularly John, a grudge and it was only a matter of time before they were charged. John Proctor was found guilty and hanged on 19 August 1692.

Mother Redcap

An elderly woman who lived in a village near Cambridge in the early part of the twentieth century and claimed to be a witch. She alleged that she was endowed with her powers by a black man after she had signed her name on a pact that he gave her. This harked back to the pacts with the devil that were such a part of witchcraft lore when witchcraft hysteria was at its height, but Redcap does not appear to have made any deal by which she gave her soul to the devil in exchange for material gain.

According to Redcap the black man had promised her familiars who would do her bidding, and certainly she appears to have been regularly accompanied by a cat, rat, mouse, toad and ferret. The old woman fared much better than those associated with witchcraft in previous generations as she was allowed to go about the even tenor of her ways, although her neighbours were quite well aware of her claims. This may well have been as her supposed powers were directed at helping others, say by healing, rather than at harming them.

Not for her was the horror of hanging or burning at the stake. She died quietly in 1926.

Anne Redfearne

One of the Pendle Witches (page 166).

Helen Rogie

One of the supposed witches involved in the witch trials in

Aberdeen in 1596, Rogie was accused of making waxen images of anyone she disliked with a view to bringing harm on them. This was an extremely common charge when seeking to establish evidence of witchcraft. *See* Aberdeen Witches, page 93.

St Osyth Witches

The St Osyth Witches were part of the accusations of witchcraft that plagued parts of Essex for many years. A village near Brightlingsea in Essex, St Osyth was the home of around fourteen witches who were tried for witchcraft at Chelmsford in 1582 (*see* Chelmsford Witches, page 111). In common with some other witch trials, the incident that sparked off this particular one was in the nature of a village quarrel that became exaggerated and embellished out of all proportion.

The person first accused was Ursula Kempe (page 152), a local woman of little means who tried to make a living from working as a nursemaid and midwife and from her skill as a healer. It was reputed that she could undo spells that had been placed on people and supposedly caused them harm. This was to be her undoing because she fell foul of one Grace Thurlowe who accused her of witchcraft with relevance to treatment for her arthritic condition.

The trial of the St Osyth Witches was noteworthy for its use of child witnesses who were well under the official age at which witnesses were allowed to give evidence, and this trend was to continue in future witch trials. Such a witness was Kempe's eight-year-old son. Partly because of her son's testimony, but mostly because she was assured that the court would treat her with clemency if she confessed, she duly confessed and, as was frequently the case with confessions of witchcraft, implicated several of her neighbours. They in turn implicated others, and eventually fourteen women stood accused. The charges were various, ranging from the relatively minor, such as preventing beer from brewing, to the major one of causing death by sorcery, twenty-four people being alleged to have died by such means.

When the trial came to an end, Kempe was sentenced to execution by hanging, as was Elizabeth Bennet (page 101). Of the others, Annis Herd was especially fortunate to be acquitted since she was charged with causing death by sorcery, a charge that usually resulted in execution.

The trial increased the witchcraft hysteria in the area and in the Chelmsford Witchcraft Trial of 1645 (*see* Chapter 2, page 33), instigated by the witch-finder Matthew Hopkins (*see* page 59), were several accused witches from St Osyth.

Salem Witches

One of the best-known mass witchcraft trials occurred in Salem, Massachusetts, from 1692 until 1693. Whilst not large by European standards the number of the accused was very great in terms of the New World. Nineteen people were found guilty and executed by hanging. It is thought that over one hundred and forty people were arrested as suspects on the say-so of a group of hysterical young girls. Of those who were not executed some avoided death on the grounds of pregnancy, some confessed to witchcraft in order to save their lives, some were reprieved, some escaped, and towards the end of the hysterical period, when people were no longer taking the girls so seriously and when spectral evidence was no longer allowed, many were acquitted. For further details *see* Chapter 2, Salem Witchcraft Trials, page 41. *See* also George Burroughs (page 110); Giles Corey (page 118); Martha Corey (page 119); Sarah Good (page 136); Sarah Osborne (page 166); Elizabeth Proctor (page 171); John Proctor (page 171); Tituba (page 185); John Willard (page 196).

Agnes Sampson

An elderly midwife, Sampson was one of those supposedly involved in the alleged coven operated by the North Berwick Witches (page 163), whose members were put on trial between 1590 and 1592, North Berwick being a town down the east coast from Edinburgh. She is noted for the detailed and sensational revelations that she made at her trial, including those involving a supposed plot against the king, James VI. Although she went on to make extravagant claims with reference to her connection with witchcraft and the devil, Sampson at first declared her innocence.

She was accused of witchcraft by Gilly Duncan (page 125), accusations by whom set off the trials of the North Berwick Witches. In her formal confession, forced out of her by torture, Duncan was moved to identify Sampson as one of her accomplices. On denying any connection with witchcraft, Sampson was ordered by the authorities to be shaved so that the telltale devil's mark could be looked for, this being an imprint supposedly left by the devil somewhere on the bodies of his followers. Just about any mark was taken as such a sign and an indication of guilt.

The searches for such a mark could be embarrassing and humiliating, and in Sampson's case the search resulted in the location of a mark in her genitals, which was declared to be a devil's mark. This being taken as clear evidence of her association with witchcraft and the devil, the next step was to submit Sampson to a series of tortures. One of these was thrawing (page 86), to which Sampson's accuser, Gilly Duncan, was also subjected. This involved jerking the victim's head violently by means of a rope. The old woman was also forced to be deprived of sleep until she confessed to her supposed misdeeds and was forced to wear a witch's bridle. The latter was a fearsome device, made of iron, that was put over the supposed witch's head and held down her tongue so that she was unable to speak, the idea being to prevent the person from speaking and so from giving voice to any curses that she might bring down on her accusers or tormentors.

In the light of this severe torture, and of the fact that the authorities threatened to repeat it, it is hardly surprising that Sampson eventually formally confessed to witchcraft. Officiating at her trial and at those of her fellow-accused was none other than the king, King James VI of Scotland, later to become James I of England. It is said that one of the reasons for his taking on such a role was that some of the accused were of noble connections.

Sampson, having once confessed, went to town on the crimes that she claimed to have committed in her role of witch. She laid claim to some of the more usual activities associated with witchcraft, including keeping a dog as her familiar, using charms to harm people and livestock and attending sabbats, orgiastic meetings of witches.

When speaking of the sabbats she went into great and lurid detail, speaking of sailing from a Hallowe'en sabbat to North

Berwick in a series of sieves and kissing the buttocks of the devil in a ceremony in a church there.

The accused then went on to tell of how she and other members of the coven set about trying to use their witchcraft to bring about the death of the king, once by raising a storm and throwing a cat with a dead man's limbs strapped to its paws into the sea in the hope that this would make the king's ship sink on its voyage to Denmark to collect his bride-to-be, once by melting a wax image of the king in a fire, and once by attempting to get hold of one his garments so that they could smear it with poison obtained from a black toad left suspended by its feet for three days.

Many were disposed to think that all this was a result of an old woman's fevered imagination, and, of course, it is highly possible that her mind had been deranged by the terrible tortures to which she had been subjected. Even the king claimed at one point that he felt that Sampson and some of the others were not telling the truth. However, he claimed to have been brought round to believing their stories when, according to him, Sampson was able to whisper to him the very words that he and his bride had said to each other on their wedding night. The king took this as positive proof of Sampson's association with witchcraft, although, since no one else heard her whispers, it is possible that this was all invented by the king so that the accused could be found guilty and suitably punished as a warning to others never to become involved in witchcraft. Probably he was also not enamoured of anyone claiming to have tried to kill him, whether in fact these claims were true.

The claims made by Sampson and her co-accused were so unlikely that the court was inclined to disbelieve them, and at one point the members of the jury voted to have the charges dismissed. This did not please the king, however, and to appease his anger the court was assembled again and Sampson and some of her co-accused were found guilty. Sampson was executed.

Alice, John and Agnes Samuel

Known sometimes as the Warboys Witches, their supposed witchcraft practices having taken place in Warboys in Huntingdonshire, the Samuel family, Alice and her husband and daughter, were all charged with witchcraft and found guilty. However, it was originally only Alice, an elderly woman in her seventies, who was involved.

The Samuels were neighbours to a family named Throckmorton who lived in Warboys. One day when Alice went to visit them one of the Throckmortons' five daughters, ten-year-old Jane, took some kind of fit. The likelihood is that this was an epileptic seizure but, of course, not much was known about seizures in those days and the girl accused Alice of having caused the fit. Someone being accused of witchcraft on the say-so of a young girl was to prove a common element in witch trials, as was the fact that one girl's historical claims could affect others. So it was with the Throckmorton girls who were soon afflicted by the same fits as their sisters.

A Cambridge doctor was sent for to find a reason for the seizures but was unable to identify any medical reason for them. This was enough for the presence of witchcraft to be suspected. It is to the credit of the Throckmorton parents that at first they dismissed the notion of their daughters' condition being the result of witchcraft and bore no ill-will towards Alice Samuel.

The condition of their daughters worsened, however, and they became desperate. They finally decided to approach Alice with the suspicions that had been aroused. Unfortunately for her, the fits of the girls grew ever more violent, as was to be the case in several later trials. The hysteria spread and soon other members of the household claimed to be affected by seizures. Again this was to become a common feature of witch trials.

It happened that the girls took to having fits only in the absence of Alice and, in an attempt to alleviate their supposed suffering, the old woman was ordered to become a permanent resident in the Throckmorton household for the time being. This was to be her undoing because, not only did they now have fits in her presence, but they began to accuse her of other deeds associated with witchcraft.

The wife of the man who owned the land inhabited by the Throckmortons came to call to see if she could do something about the undue influence that Alice was claimed to have over the girls. This was none other than Lady Cromwell, grandmother of Oliver Cromwell, who was to become Lord Protector of England. She is said to have cut off and burned some of Alice's hair in attempt to destroy any spell that she might have put on the girls. This appeared to have no effect on the girls' fits.

Shortly afterwards Lady Cromwell was to make a claim that did Alice's case no good whatsoever. She alleged that she had had a terrible nightmare in which she was attacked by Alice Samuel and her cat, cats being commonly held to be familiars of witches. The nightmare affected her so badly that she became ill and died some fifteen months later. On her death, when suspicions against Alice were rife, it was claimed that when Lady Cromwell had cut off part of her hair the old woman had asked her why she was treating her thus when she had not done her any harm as yet. It was the 'as yet' that did it. People began to speculate that this had been a threat of future harm.

Meanwhile Alice, not knowing how else to stop the girls' fits, ordered them to stop having seizures. This they did, and this was taken as further proof of Alice's involvement in their cause. By this time Alice was extremely distressed and confused. She went to visit the local minister and confessed that she must indeed be a witch if she was making the girls' fits happen. Having taken time to think about the situation and to recover her senses a bit, she withdrew the confession, only to have the Throckmorton girls start having fits all over again.

This was now taken as proof that the elderly Samuel woman did indeed have a magical influence over the girls, and she was questioned about her activities by two local justices of the peace and the Bishop of Lincoln. Again, as was hardly surprising, given her age and the amount of stress to which she had been subjected, she was moved to confess her guilt and even gave some details of witchlike activities.

Accusations of witchcraft had a nasty habit of seeming to be infectious, and soon other members of the local community were supposedly recollecting magical things done by Alice or her husband or daughter. For example, they claimed that livestock had been harmed, and even killed, by them.

Agnes, the daughter of Alice, refused to admit to any association with witchcraft but she was found guilty with her parents and all three were hanged in April 1593. It was a terrible illustration of what the hysteria of young girls can bring about.

After the executions the seizures suffered by the Throckmorton girls mysteriously cleared up. In line with the law, the property of the condemned witches was forfeited. It became the property of Henry, Lord Cromwell, and he used the money to set up a fund to be used to finance the preaching in Huntingdon of an annual sermon against witchcraft, the last of these sermons being given as late as 1814.

Sathan

The name of the cat who was the familiar of first one of the Chelmsford Witches (page 111), Elizabeth Francis (page 130) and then another, Agnes Waterhouse (page 191).

Michael Scott

Scott was renowned for his scholarship and, although he spoke out against necromancy and magic, is reputed himself to have been particularly adept at the art of sorcery. Little is known of his early life except that he was born in the second half of the twelfth century, possible in Balweary, near Kirkcaldy in Fife, Scotland. His family are assumed to have been fairly affluent. He was sent to Oxford to study and after this travelled extensively

Mother Shipton

The name given to a woman who was born, probably around 1488, as Ursula Southeil in Knaresborough in Yorkshire to Agatha Southeil, a young pauper who died giving birth to Ursula in a cave. Agatha was credited with the power of clairvoyance, healing and the ability to cast spells on people and animals.

Ursula was said to have inherited her mother's skills and her extremely unattractive physical appearance seemed to confirm this in some people's eyes, the archetypal witch being an elderly, ugly old woman. Ursula may have been ugly but she was not old at the time she first became associated with strange happenings. From her childhood weird incidents are alleged to have occurred when she was in the vicinity, such as furniture moving around and houses being ransacked without any sign of anyone being present.

Because she was so strange looking and because of her reputation, people were afraid of Ursula, and it was said that those who made fun of her rather grotesque appearance were likely to be harmed in some way. Although she was widely assumed to have the ability to bewitch people, it was as a prophetess and clairvoyant that she was best known. Despite her unfortunate appearance, she married at quite a young age, twenty-four, a carpenter by the name of Tobias Shipton, although, apart from this basic fact, little is known of him. She thus changed her name to Shipton and became known as Mother Shipton.

Mother Shipton is credited with a whole range of prophecies. She was well known in her lifetime and even better known after various books of her prophecies were written, although it is likely that some of her supposed prophecies were the invention of these later writers, who included Richard Head who published a book of her predictions in 1667.

Her prophecies mainly took the form of rhymes and riddles that could be variously interpreted, and the events that she is alleged to have foretold include the Great Fire of London, the invention of the motor car, the California Gold

Rush, the building of Crystal Palace in London, World War II and the women's liberation movement. One prophecy that she appears to have got right was the one that she made regarding her own death. She died about the age of seventy around 1560 and was buried outside York, although her supposed association with witchcraft prevented her from being buried on hallowed ground. Her fame lives on today and the cave where she was born is a tourist attraction.

It is as well for Mother Shipton that she lived when she did. Had she lived later when the country was in the grip of witchcraft hysteria she is unlikely to have lived so long. She just missed the legislation passed in England against witchcraft in 1563 in the reign of Elizabeth I.

Ellen Smith

One of the Chelmsford Witches (page 111), who was tried in the second wave of witch trials in Chelmsford, which took place in 1579. She was charged with causing the death of a child by means of sorcery, made a formal confession to using witchcraft and was hanged at the same time as Elizabeth Francis (page 130).

Elizabeth Sowthern

With Anne Whittle, Sowthern was one of the most prominent of the Pendle Witches (page 166).

Stamford Witches

In the spring of 1692, around the time of the hysteria that surrounded the infamous Salem Witches, some women were accused of witchcraft in the town of Stamford in Connecticut. The charges were brought by a young girl, Katherine Branch, a servant girl in the employment of one Daniel Westcot. She first of all complained of fits. Such fits, which were very probably a result of epilepsy, were frequently associated with witchcraft at the time.

At the same time she complained about experiencing a pricking feeling in her chest when she was gathering herbs. She claimed to have seen a cat who had promised her good things if she would go with it, and later she alleged to have been approached by ten cats threatening to kill her for having revealed to others what had happened to her during her herb-gathering.

She continued to have fits on a regular basis for about two weeks and claimed also to be suffering from hallucinations. The wife of Daniel Westcot was a sensible woman and was not disposed to believe her servant's claims that witchcraft was involved. She sent for a midwife to see if she could diagnose or cure Branch's condition. At first the midwife thought that the girl's fits had some natural cause and subjected her to various treatments, such as bleeding. When none of these was effective the midwife came to the conclusion that there was witchcraft involved.

Then Branch began to names. These included Elizabeth Clauson (page 114), Mercy Disborough (page 123), Goody Miller, Hannah and Mary Harvey, and Mary Staples. Of these, Goody Miller panicked and fled to the colony of New York in order to avoid arrest. The two Harveys and Staples were held under suspicion of witchcraft. As was common in witchcraft trials, people were invited to come forward and provide information that would testify to their guilt. Unusually, not many did. Indeed, only two people offered testimonies against them and they were all three acquitted.

Of the other two, Disborough was tried and found not guilty and Clauson was tried, found guilty and sentenced to death but reprieved on appeal.

John Stewart

The person who was responsible for the authorities being able to arrest Margaret Barclay (page 98) for witchcraft in connection with the running aground of her brother-in-law's ship. He claimed to have powers of clairvoyance and claimed to know that the ship had been lost before evidence of this was established. It was his claim that he had been asked by Barclay for a curse with which to bring down the ship and that he had seen Barclay and accomplices making clay figures of her brother-in-law and fellow-sailors and throwing them into the sea so that the men might suffer the fate of being lost at sea.

It was sadly a common occurrence for people to try to implicate others when they were accused of witchcraft, whether or not this was part of a forced confession. The authorities had heard of Stewart's claimed clairvoyance in connection with the loss of the ship and arrested him as a witch. He in turn accused Margaret Barclay. Barclay succeed in escaping torture but not death. Fearing the torture and the terrible death he would be likely to have to endure he succeeded in somehow freeing himself from his shackles and took his own life by hanging himself in his cell.

Tituba

One of the Salem Witches (page 174), Tituba was the servant of the local minister, Samuel Parris, and one of the earliest of the women in Salem to be charged. Tituba was from the West Indies, she and her husband, John, having been taken to Salem as slaves by Parris who had been a merchant in Barbados. They were given the surname Indian but this is unlikely to have been their real name.

Tituba's duties including looking after the nine-year-old daughter of the house, Elizabeth Parris, and her eleven-year-old cousin, Abigail Williams. It is thought highly likely that Tituba regaled the girls with tales of her native country, including stories of voodoo. Apparently the girls and some of their friends then became interested in the occult and started dabbling in such activities as fortune-telling before the onset of their hysterical fits. Had it not been for the advent of Tituba to Salem, it is a distinct possibility that the Salem witchcraft hysteria would never have taken place.

It might be thought inevitable that Tituba was one of the girls' first accused. She knew too much about them and so was a likely target. In addition, being an exotic stranger and a poor one, in the community people would be unlikely to leap to her defence. Tituba was moved to confess to witchcraft, probably because, like others, she had been assured that a confession would result in a reprieve or at least save her from the gallows.

Such an assurance did not always bear fruit in witchcraft trials, but in fact Tituba's life was spared in the light of her confession and she was sent to prison for an indefinite period. However, since it was part of the ethos of witchcraft trials that the accused had to pay for the expenses of the trial, whether they lived or die, Tituba was eventually sold as a slave to recoup the trial costs.

Tituba's imagination was obviously at work in the course

of her confession. She claimed to have gone to coven meetings with Sarah Good and Sarah Osborne and that there was a coven in Massachusetts led by a tall, white-haired man dressed in black, later assumed to be George Burroughs (page 110). The latter, she claimed, had forced her to sign the devil's pact, and she claimed to have seen nine other names on this. This naming of names of others was a common feature of confessions in witchcraft trials

Mary Trembles

One of the Exeter Witches (page 127), who, with her co-accused, Susanna Edwards (page 126) and Temperance Lloyd (page 156), was accused of witchcraft and executed by hanging in August 1682. She seems to have been the least strong of the three, allegedly having been recruited to the coven by Edwards and having wept on her way to the gallows after having been found guilty.

Trèves Witches

The German town of Trèves, situated in the Rhineland and now called Trier, was the centre of much witchcraft hysteria in the later part of the sixteenth century. The area had been subject to several misfortunes and was in a mood to blame these misfortunes on any available scapegoat. At the time witchcraft hysteria was affecting Luxembourg and this soon spread, becoming widespread in Trèves in 1582.

The campaign of terrible persecution (*see* Chapter 2, Witchcraft Trials, page 32) that raged resulted in the deaths of six thousand accused witches between the years of 1587 and 1594. It was remarked upon by a commentator that many of these executed Trèves Witches were extremely affluent, the implication being that their wealth had been a factor in the accusations laid against them, since those found guilty of witchcraft had their possessions confiscated.

One of the accused Trèves Witches was Dietrich Flade, originally a civil judge officiating at witchcraft trials. The original charge against him was that he was too lenient in his judgements. Found guilty of this charge, he was removed from the post. Later he himself was accused of witchcraft, found guilty and executed. Such was the hysteria of the times.

Charles Walton

Charles Walton (1871–1945) lived in the village of Lower Quinton in Warwickshire and in this area was popularly held to be a witch. He is perhaps best remembered for his murder.

This area of England had long had an association with witchcraft and belief in the art was likely to survive there longer than in other areas. The Rollright Stones, a megalithic stone circle in the locality, were long thought to be associated with witches and a gathering place for covens. Indeed there is a legend that maintains that the stones were originally a Danish king and his army who were turned to stone by a local witch.

Walton was an agricultural worker who lived with his niece, Edith, and was a recluse. He was regarded as being a skilled clairvoyant and appeared to have strange powers with regard to birds. It is said that he was able to converse with birds and to direct them to do as he wished, having the same skill with some animals, but on a latter scale. He bred large natterjack toads in his garden, which was quite likely to call witchcraft to mind since toads played quite a large part in witchcraft lore. His presumed association with witchcraft was also said to take him at night to the Rollright Stones, supposedly to watch witches performing their rituals.

It was alleged that he acquired his prophetic skills when he was a boy after encountering a black dog three nights running on nearby Meon Hill. On the third night the black dog is said to have changed into a headless woman. The next day his sister died. Walton became extremely introverted and developed powers of clairvoyance.

On 14 February 1945 Walton set out to do some work in the fields of a farmer whose land lay near Meon Hill, carrying a pitchfork and billhook for use in his work. The farmer saw him at midday but he failed to return home at his appointed time. A small search party was got up to look for the old man and its members came upon his body lying at the foot of a willow tree. His body had been cruelly mutilated, his pitchfork having been thrust so violently through his neck that it had nearly beheaded him and his billhook having been used to make a cross-shaped wound in his chest. Not surprisingly his face held a look of terror.

It was difficult to account for Walton's murder, since he was very much a man who kept himself to himself. The local people suspected that it was his supposed connection with witchcraft that had led to his death. This suspicion was heightened by the fact that a black dog had been found hanged on Meon Hill a few days after the old man's death.

The Scotland Yard detective Robert Fabian was put in charge of the investigation and probably assumed that the crime could be solved relatively quickly, given the size of the village. His investigations were hampered by the silence and lack of cooperation that he encountered among the villagers. Fabian's men took four thousand statements and around thirty samples of clothing, hair and blood but the murderer of Walton remained unidentified. It was assumed that the death was in some way connected with witchcraft but nothing was ever proved.

There was a suggestion that Walton's death might be what is now known as a copycat crime. In 1875 in a neighbouring village called Long Compton an elderly woman suspected of witchcraft, Anne Turner, was murdered by a mentally retarded man called John Haywood because he thought that she had bewitched him. The method of murder was the same in both cases. Turner, too, had been pinned to the ground with a pitchfork and had had her chest slashed in the shape of a cross.

Another theory was that Walton was the victim of an attack by someone who thought he had been bewitched by him and who was intent on removing the spell by a method known as scoring above the breath, a procedure well known around the time of the witchcraft hysteria. In order to destroy a spell by scoring the breath the bewitched person had to make the witch bleed above the nose or mouth.

A third suggested possibility was that Walton's murder was connected with a pagan ritual. The date of his death, 14 February, was the date on which the druids undertook blood rituals in order to ensure abundant crops. The crops of the previous year had been poor, and it was thought that someone might have come up with such a solution to ensure fertility. The ritual involved draining the blood of a dead man or woman into the soil.

It was suggested that perhaps Walton had been selected to have his blood used because he had been accused of using witchcraft to bring about poor crops. He was alleged to have taken some of the natterjack toads that he bred and harnessed them to toy ploughs so that they could run across the fields and blight the soil.

There may have been some more rational reason behind Walton's death. None was ever found, however, and the identity of the perpetrator of the crime was never discovered.

Wapping Witch

A name given to Joan Peterson (page 169), who was found guilty of witchcraft and hanged at Tyburn in April 1652.

Warboys Witches

A name given to three members of a family called Samuel who were accused of practising witchcraft in Warboys in Huntingdonshire and brought to trial at Huntingdon in 1593. The case had many of the elements that were to become typical of witch trials in later years when witchcraft hysteria reigned. *See* Alice, John and Agnes Samuel, page 178.

Agnes Waterhouse

One of the first of the Chelmsford Witches to be accused, Waterhouse was a peasant woman in her early sixties from Hatfield Peverel. She was to be the first of many in the area to be accused and tried. She was charged with the killing of a man name William Fynee, it being alleged that she had used sorcery to affect him with a wasting disease. She was tried by no less a person than the Attorney-General, Sir Gilbert Gerard. This indicated how seriously witchcraft was taken and was to influence the thinking of others in later trials.

Children were used to testify in court, uncorroborated

statements of guilt were accepted and, fatally for Waterhouse, the devil's mark (page 254) was found upon her. Waterhouse confessed and was hanged, it not being in her favour that her cat, supposedly her familiar and accomplice in Fynee's death, was named Sathan. This cat had been given to Waterhouse by Elizabeth Francis (page 130) who was also charged with witchcraft, as was Waterhouse's daughter Joan Waterhouse (page 192).

Joan Waterhouse

It was common to assume that witchcraft ran in families, and it was quite usual for members of the same family, particularly mother and daughter, to be accused of being witches. Thus it was in the case of the Waterhouse family from Hatfield Peverel in Essex. Joan Waterhouse was the daughter of Agnes Waterhouse (page 191) and, like her mother, was one of the early Chelmsford Witches (page 111). Aged eighteen she was not accused of the same crime as her mother but was charged with having caused damage to the limbs of a twelve-year-old girl, Agnes Brown, it being very common for children to be accusers in charges of witchcraft.

The girl claimed that a black dog, allegedly Sathan, a black cat owned by Agnes Waterhouse, in an assumed shape, had been present at the time of the injuries. Fate, not to mention the authorities, was kinder to the daughter than the mother and Joan was acquitted.

Thomas Weir

A military man, who became extremely eccentric as he grew older, Weir voluntarily confessed to witchcraft at the age of seventy. He had seen distinguished service as a soldier in the

Parliamentarian army in Ireland in 1641 and became commander of the Edinburgh City Guard in 1649. He was extremely religious and was a much respected senior figure in the Presbyterian church in Edinburgh. His history of extreme piety made all the more extraordinary his claims of witchcraft.

In the light of his previous character no one was inclined to believe his confession and assumed that he was mentally ill. However, doctors were duly sent for and they gave it as their professional opinion that he was sane. In the light of their findings the Provost of Edinburgh felt obliged to arrest Weir. He lived with his sister and, since his confession had also implicated her, she too was arrested.

They were both brought to trial in April 1670, but there was no mention of witchcraft in the charges, since it would have been an embarrassment to the Presbyterian church to have one of their senior figures accused of sorcery and of consorting with the devil. Weir had in fact confessed to sorcery but he had also confessed to incest, adultery and sodomy, and it was with these that he was charged – incest with his sister, adultery with his sister's servant girl and sodomy with horses and cattle. These were hardly charges befitting a man of such piety but clearly the church members thought that anything was better than witchcraft.

His sister by this time was in a mental state that was even worse than that of Weir. She confessed to having sold her soul to the devil and to having kept a familiar that enabled her to spin yarn at three or four times faster than the average woman. She also maintained that her brother did practise witchcraft and used a carved wooden staff that he carried everywhere to work his spells.

The court confined itself to finding both accused guilty of incest and bestiality and set aside the question of witchcraft. The accused were both condemned to death. Weir was strangled and burnt at the stake and his sister was hanged the following day.

Many people charged with witchcraft were elderly people and many of them were women. It is likely that many of these were in some way mentally unbalanced. Certainly it seems almost certain, despite the doctor's findings, that Weir was not entirely sane.

Jane Wenham

Wenham was the last person to be sentenced to death by an English court on charges of witchcraft, although the sentence was never in fact carried out. The sentence of execution established by the court had been passed against the wish of the judge, Sir John Powell. He was able to delay the death of the condemned woman until he was able to secure a royal pardon for her and obtain her freedom.

Nicknamed the Wise Woman of Walkerne, in recognition of the fact that she was an inhabitant of Walkerne in Hertfordshire, Wenham had long been labelled locally as a witch, although she became extremely angry if anyone accused her of having anything to do with witchcraft. Wenham was more formally accused of witchcraft in 1712 when a local servant girl, Anne Thorne, who was employed by the local minister, claimed that the woman had caused her to have fits and to vomit pins. These were standard charges in witch trials, especially when made by girls or young women. Thorne further accused Wenham of causing her to suffer from hallucinations in which she saw demons in the form of cats and of using her magic to force her to run half-a-mile, despite the fact that she was suffering from an injured leg.

It often took just one accusation of witchcraft for a whole series to follow. Soon other local people were supposedly remembering incidents that damned Wenham. She was duly arrested and formal proceedings begun. She was searched for evidence of the devil's mark (page 254), but Wenham was lucky not have any such mark identified on her body.

This did not do her much good, however, for at this point she decided to make a full confession. Admittedly, she claimed to be a white witch, practising her art only in the cause of good. She seemed fully convinced that she had magical powers that she had probably used in healing, but it was not white magic that was of concern to her accusers. It was the black art in which they were interested, and soon they charged her with conversing with the devil in the shape of a cat. Then further supposed evidence against her was brought to court. This took the form of some ointment that was found under her pillow. Bizarrely, it was judged by the prosecution to have been made from human fat.

This was enough evidence against her, and she was found guilty and sentenced to death. As has been described above, she was saved from execution by the intervention of the judge. There was such strong feeling against her in some quarters, however, that she was unable to return to her cottage and resume her normal life. She did not fare too badly because she was saved from a life of wandering when a local man who was sorry for her provided her with a cottage in Hartingfordbury. There she lived until her death in 1730.

The case attracted a great deal of public interest – and not just at local level. It resulted in much debate on the subject of witchcraft, and several pamphlets about the Wenham affair were published.

Anne Whittle

With Elizabeth Sowthern (page 183), Whittle was one of the most prominent of the Pendle Witches (page 166).

John Willard

One of the Salem Witches (page 174), Willard was a local farmer and a deputy constable. In the latter post he had been responsible for issuing the initial writs against the accused witches. He became convinced, however, that the real guilty parties were the hysterical girl accusers and made his views known. It was a foregone conclusion that the girls would take their revenge on him and, realising this, he fled. Unfortunately for him, he was captured a few days later and charged following accusations made against him by Mrs Putnam and some of the girls. He was unable to recite the Lord's Prayer faultlessly, probably because he was nervous. This was held to be clear evidence of an association with witchcraft and he was convicted and hanged on 19 August 1692.

Christine Wilson

Also known as the Dalkeith Witch, Dalkeith being a town near Edinburgh, Wilson was accused of witchcraft and sent for trial in 1661. The noteworthy thing about her trial is that the authorities used a method known as bier right as a test of witchcraft.

This test was used in cases where witchcraft was alleged to

have resulted in murder and involved getting the accused witch to touch the dead body of the alleged victim. If the corpse began to bleed it was taken as absolute proof that the accused was a witch. Unfortunately for Wilson, when she laid her hand on the wound that had killed her supposed victim it is said to have begun to bleed profusely. She was therefore declared to be guilty without further ado.

The bier right test did not originate with witchcraft trials. It was originally used in murder trials, it being part of folk legend that a corpse that had been the victim of murder would begin to bleed when it was in the presence of the murderer, or at least when he or she touched it.

Janet Wishart

One of the supposed witches involved in the witchcraft trials in Aberdeen in 1596, Wishart was suspected of murdering one man by magic and causing severe illness in another. She was also charged with removing body parts from a corpse of someone who was hanged while it was still on the gallows, the said body parts supposedly being for use in her pursuit of witchcraft. *See* Aberdeen Witches, page 93.

Elizabeth Woodville

The eldest daughter of Sir Richard Woodville and Jacquetta, Duchess of Bedford, Elizabeth Woodville (*c.* 1437–92) married the English king, Edward IV in 1464 in a secret marriage ceremony. There were many people who were against this marriage since it was deemed to be politically unsuitable. There were attempts made to discredit it and to invalidate it.

Woodville, who had previously been married to Sir John Grey but had been widowed when he was killed in battle in 1461, first met the king in Whittlebury Forest. A rumour was started by those wishing to invalidate the marriage that she had deliberately set out to ensnare the king and that she and her mother, the Duchess of Bedford, had made use of witchcraft in the process. When the king was imprisoned by the Earl of Warwick after an uprising in 1469, the rumours grew more persistent, since the king was not there to challenge them.

A man called Thomas Wake produced a figure of a knight cast in lead that had a wire tied round it. He claimed that this had been fashioned by the duchess as part of her scheme to ensnare the king for her daughter. Another man, John Daunger, said that two more figures had been fashioned and that one had represented the king and the other the duchess's daughter.

Wake made formal charges against the duchess, and the case went to court in 1470. By that time the king was out of prison and Daunger, nervous of incurring the king's wrath, retracted his statement about the figures and denied that he had suggested that the duchess was involved in witchcraft. This left the case somewhat short on evidence and the duchess was acquitted.

However, complications arose on the death of Edward IV in 1483. The late king's son, Edward, was in line to become the next king as Edward V. If the marriage of his mother, Elizabeth Woodville, to Edward IV could be invalidated then he would not ascend the throne, being illegitimate. Instead the throne would pass to Richard of Gloucester, brother of Edward IV. It was obviously in Richard's interest to have the marriage invalidated.

It is said that Richard then turned rumours of witchcraft

towards Elizabeth Woodville and towards the mistress of the late king, Jane Shore. Richard had a withered arm that had been in such a condition since birth. He chose conveniently to forget this, however, and accused Woodville and Shore of causing the damage to his arm by means of witchcraft. Many knew that this condition had been present at his birth but they were too terrified to say so.

Shore was imprisoned in the Tower of London and all her property was confiscated. She was also compelled to do penance by walking barefoot through the streets of London wearing only a smock. Woodville, who was Richard's main target, fled for refuge to Westminster, taking with her her youngest son. Richard then crowned himself king as Richard III and later imprisoned the boy who should have been Edward V and his brother in the Tower of London, where they were to die in mysterious circumstances.

Elizabeth Woodville had tragically lost both her sons, but she did at least acquire the title of dowager queen when Henry VII ascended the throne of England in 1485. She died in Bermondsey Abbey in 1492.

Elizabeth Wright

The mother of Alice Goodridge (page 136) who was accused with her daughter of witchcraft largely because she had given her a dog, the dog being claimed to be a witch's familiar. It was very common to suppose that witchcraft ran in families and very often a mother or daughter would be charged as well as the accused. Goodridge died in jail before she could face the death sentence but history does not record what happened to Wright.

John Wrightson

Known as the Wise Man of Stokesley, he was known throughout the area south of Durham and around north Yorkshire at
the beginning of the nineteenth century for his powers as a
white witch. These supposed powers were used by him in
various ways that were beneficial to those with whom he
came in contact. For example, people sought his help in finding lost or stolen possessions and to cure sick livestock and
they came from miles around so to do. It was his contention
that his magical powers were effective only when he was fasting.

Alice (Alse) Young

One of the Connecticut Witches (page 117), Young was the
first person to be executed after anti-witchcraft legislation was
passed in the state in 1642. She was hanged in May 1647.

Chapter 4

Witchcraft Connections

There were many things traditionally associated with witchcraft, whether these were living creatures, plants, objects, or rituals. Some of the best known of these are categorised below.

Creatures and Deities

bat

Because of its dark colour and its nocturnal habits bats were often associated with evil and death. In some cultures they were seen as harbingers of death and witches were once popularly thought to be able to change themselves into bats for ease of gaining access to buildings. It was thought in some areas of Europe that a house might be protected against witchcraft if a dead bat were nailed on the outside of a house, such as a window or shed, provided that the bat had been carried three times round the outside of the house before being killed.

The blood of the bat was allegedly used in witches' potions, particularly in the potion known as flying ointment, which was an aid to the witch's ability to fly on her broomstick. Bat's blood was also sometimes used in the celebration of the rite known as black mass (page 283).

bee

The bee, more specifically the queen bee, had an unusual role in the European witchcraft trials organised by the Inquisition. The interrogators were always on the lookout for some reason for accused witches being able to withstand torture without making their confessions which were so vital to the legal system. One of these alleged, and extremely unlikely, reasons was that, if the accused witch swallowed a queen bee before being arrested by the authorities, he or she would be able to sustain the torment of torture and the rigours of the trial without confessing to involvement in witchcraft.

blackbird

The colour black from early times has been associated with death and also with evil. Thus any creature of that colour was likely to be suspect. This being the case, it was almost inevitable that a blackbird would be numbered among those creatures likely to be regarded as a witch's familiar (page 210). The fact that this was so points to the difficulty that the accused witch had in proving that he or she did not have a familiar. Even today, when chemicals in herbicides and pesticides have taken their toll of wildlife, blackbirds are by no means an uncommon sight. In the days of rampant witchcraft hysteria blackbirds would have been even more common a sight, always popping into gardens in search of food and thus condemning any old woman whose garden they chose to potential charges of witchcraft.

black cat *see* CAT.

black dog

As has been indicated above, black has long been regarded as the colour of death and evil. A dog of whatever colour was always a likely candidate as an alleged witch's familiar (page 210), although the dog was not so closely associated with witchcraft as its traditional enemy, the cat (page 203). An old woman, especially an unattractive one behaving strangely, who lived alone and kept a pet for company, at the height of the witchcraft hysteria, especially in England, was at grave risk of being accused of being involved in witchcraft and of keeping a familiar.

Her predicament was even worse if the dog was black in colour for that was thought to be a favourite shape of the devil. It was alleged that the devil often assumed the shape of a large black dog at witches' orgiastic gatherings or sabbats. Tradition had it that he most commonly turned himself into a dog when he adopted a suitable position for receiving an obscene kiss or a kiss on the buttocks from his devoted followers.

boar

This was one of several animal shapes alleged to be favoured by the devil, particularly if the boar was black in colour, the colour black being traditionally associated with evil as well as death. The devil in the shape of a boar, which was held to be a very virile creature, featured in many supposed confessions from accused witches.

cat

Throughout the ages the cat has been a favourite household pet, often being a companion to someone living alone. This made it practically a certainty to be identified as a familiar (page 210) of an accused witch, a demon that would help her work her magic. As was the case with other creatures suspected of being familiars, an accused witch did not actually have to own a cat for her to be accused of keeping one as a familiar. One chancing to pass her door, go into her garden, rub against her, etc, was enough.

Any cat was suspect but a black cat was exceptionally so, since black cats from earliest times were associated with the supernatural. In this respect cultures adopted ambivalent attitudes towards the black cat. Some saw it as a force for good, a symbol of good luck and healing, while others viewed it as a portent of bad luck. The ancient Egyptians regarded it as sacred.

As has been mentioned above, it was popularly thought that many witches kept cats as familiars, sometimes allegedly being rewarded with drops of their mistress's blood for their part in helping the witches to cause death, damage and injury. It was also thought that cats as familiars were handed on from generation to generation and sometimes from friend to friend.

Cats have long been valued for their companionship. However, at times of witchcraft hysteria people were nervous of being near a cat, fearing that it might be a demon in disguise. They felt that it might be a witches' familiar spying on them and listening in to their conversations with a view to causing them harm. Because of their association with witchcraft cats were often cruelly treated. It was not unusual for them to be attacked or killed and cats whose owners had been convicted as witches were particularly at risk. They were often burned alive, especially in continental Europe.

Cats were feared not only because they were suspected of being familiars of witches but because it was suspected that they might even be witches who had taken the shape of cats. Witches were traditionally thought to be able to change shape and the cat was a favourite shape. If a cat was injured in some way, whether deliberately or accidentally, and an old crone in the village appeared with a wound in the same area of the body, it was automatically assumed that she was a witch who had been injured when in the form of the cat. It was popularly held that witches could change into cats nine times in their lives. The devil also was traditionally supposed to adopt the shape of a cat from time to time, thus preventing some people from harming a cat in case it was the devil in disguise and took reprisals on his attacker.

Thus it was difficult to decide whether a cat was a simple feline companion, a familiar, a witch or a devil. One test was devised to determine which cats were entirely innocent. They were put into a bowl of holy water and observed to see if they would try to escape. It was thought that those cats that were witches in disguise would try to escape from the presence of the holy water since witches avoided all things associated with God. This was not a very reliable test as most cats hate water and would probably try to escape.

Thus, just as many innocent people died during the reign of witchcraft hysteria so did many cats.

cock

The cock in many cultures is associated with light and in some is considered to be a force for good. Because of the bird's associations with concepts that were the opposite of the concepts associated with witchcraft, darkness and evil, it was popularly believed during the periods of witchcraft hysteria that witches sacrificed cocks as an insult to God, who was also associated with light and goodness. The crowing of the cock at dawn heralded the reappearance of light after a period of darkness and was a sign to witches that they must bring an end to their orgiastic gatherings or sabbats.

Witches were also alleged to use cocks in storm-raising, a practice that they were supposed to indulge in with a view to sinking ships at sea or destroying crops on land. Supposedly they sacrificed the birds over their cauldrons as they wove the relevant spells.

crow

The crow, like several other black creatures, has through the ages often been treated with suspicion. The bird, like the raven (page 218), was often seen as an omen of disaster and often of death and so was avoided where possible. Its specific role in witchcraft was as a familiar (page 210), people imagining that it was a demon in the shape of crow that flew around carrying out its mistress's orders and helping her work her harmful magic.

demon

Originally in pre-Christian cultures and in non-Christian cultures the word demon could be applied to a spirit, whether good or evil. Christianity, however, characterised them as being evil spirits and servants of the devil. Demons thus came to be depicted as having the same kind of shape as the devil but in miniature, although they were seen as having the ability to adopt any shape they chose at will. By this means were they able to spread their evil and cause death and destruction.

The study of demonology was once a subject that occupied the attention of many scholars. According to these experts demons were divided into a complex system of hierarchies. There were thought to be many thousands of demons, most of whom belonged to the minor hierarchies.

Ashtaroth

The best known and most major of the demons included Ashtaroth. He was associated with science and secrets and was thought to be useful in rituals relating to divination. Supposedly he gave off a terrible stench. Ashtaroth was linked with witchcraft for his alleged role in demonic possession, being one of the senior demons supposedly involved in the possession of the Loudun nuns.

Asmodeus

Another well-known and major demon is Asmodeus. He was associated with rage, revenge, lust and lechery, and was regarded as the demon most likely to be at the heart of any demonic possession of a sexual nature. It was said that if witches and sorcerers successfully conjured him up he could help them attack or destroy their enemies.

Beelzebub

Another major and powerful demon was Beelzebub. He was regarded as being the prince of demons and was known as the Lord of the Flies, because he often adopted the shape of a fly when he made an appearance.

He was traditionally linked with witchcraft in that he was thought to reign over sabbats. This was appropriate since he was associated with gluttony and orgies and supposedly copulated with the witches in the course of the sabbats. His name was chanted by witches at sabbats and at black masses (page 283). Like Ashtaroth, he was said to have been involved in the demonic possession of the Loudun nuns.

Belial

Another major demon was Belial. His name is sometimes used as a synonym for Satan, but as a demon he was associated with treachery and lies and with the creation of wickedness in humankind, especially when this wickedness was associated with sexual perversion, lust or lechery. He was considered to be not only exceptionally evil but exceptionally, and deceptively, beautiful in appearance.

Demons generally were associated with witchcraft in at least two respects. They were supposedly given the role of helpers to witches after the latter had taken allegiance to their master, the devil. In order not to advertise their evil presence, the demons took the form of creatures whose presence would not cause suspicion. These commonly included cats, dogs, hares, rabbits, toads and ravens. Such demonic witches' assistants were known as familiars.

demonic possession

Many cases of supposed witchcraft during the height of the witchcraft hysteria involved what was known as demonic possession. Nowadays cases that supposedly involved this phenomenon are thought to have been the result of deception or hysteria or instances of epilepsy or schizophrenia.

Innocent people were supposedly possessed by demons at a witch's request, and under the influence of the demons they would begin to behave in a way that was not at all in keeping with their own personalities. For example, people who were renowned for their quietness, piety and chastity might start acting in an extremely noisy, wild and lewd way. Often the victim's features took on horrible, distorted expressions and their voices became rasping or guttural. It was thought that witches could transmit demons by means of potions or foods, especially those foods, such as apples, that were common and seemed harmless.

The established cure for demonic possession was exorcism. During this exercise, priests or ministers would attempt to get the demon to leave the victim's body by calling on God and the saints to release the person from the evil presence. Sometimes the victim was physically beaten in order to force out the demon.

devil

The devil, also known as Satan or Lucifer, known to Christians as the archenemy of God, became associated with witchcraft in the Middle Ages when the idea came into being that witches worshipped the devil, not God. He remained associated with witchcraft for a long time but is not linked to modern witchcraft.

In medieval times the devil was regarded as being a real being and, like demons, he was credited with the ability of changing shape at will. Consorting with the devil was a common charge laid at the door of someone accused of witchcraft. Many confessions, often extracted from accused witches by means of standard questions and in some cases by torture, referred to the devil making a physical appearance. He was said often to take the form of a dark man dressed in black but sometimes he seemed to prefer animal disguises and appeared to the witches in the form of a black dog, a wolf, a goat or toad.

Witches supposedly took an oath of allegiance to the devil, many by the signing of a devil's pact in their own blood. In return he promised them increased magical powers and a familiar (page 210), a demon in the shape of a dog, cat, hare, etc, as an assistant. He also allegedly used to mark the bodies of his initiates in some way, the mark being known as a devil's mark. Such a mark was zealously searched for by investigators on the bodies of accused witches and just about any mark could be claimed to be a devil's mark.

He allegedly frequently put in an appearance at sabbats, and many witches confessed to having sexual intercourse with him. Part of a witch's initiation supposedly involved kissing the devil's buttocks. For the purpose of such a ceremony it was said that the devil often took the shape of an animal, such as a big black dog or a boar.

dog *see* BLACK DOG.

familiar

The witch's familiar was a common feature of witchcraft in England and Scotland, although not in mainland Europe. In England in 1604 under the tenets of the Witchcraft Act it was made a felony 'to consult, covenant with, entertain, employ, feed or reward any evil and wicked spirit'. Familiars became extremely important in witchcraft trials when the notorious witch-finder Matthew Hopkins was zealously trying to bring charges of witchcraft against as many people as possible. In those times the possession of a cat was enough to have the owner charged with suspected witchcraft.

The familiar was regarded as being a minor demon assigned by the devil to a witch to help her or him to carry out acts of magic and generally act as an assistant in return for vowing allegiance to him. Witchcraft was essentially a secret business and questions would have been asked if the demons had appeared in their allegedly usual guise, the traditional shape of the devil but in miniature. In order not to attract attention, therefore, the familiars changed shape and became creatures that would not arouse comment.

Many familiars supposedly took the shape of household pets, black cats being an exceptional favourite but dogs were also popular, as were several wild animals, such as hares, toads, rabbits, mice, and sometimes weasels and hedgehogs. Birds, such as blackbirds, crows, ravens, and even insects, were also suspected of being demons in disguise. Some witches supposedly had several familiars and it was possible to inherit a familiar or be given one by a fellow-witch. Familiars were thought to be able to adopt more than one shape and to be able to disappear at will.

Witches were allegedly very appreciative of their familiars and their help and rewarded them by taking good care of them. A special reward was said to take the form of drops of the witch's blood, sometimes sucked either from a finger, a protuberance on the skin or even a supernumerary nipple. Familiars sucking blood were thought to leave marks on the witch's skin, and evidence of such marks was carefully searched for during examination of an accused witch. Some witches were said to baptise their familiars and to give them odd names, totally unlike usual Christian names.

The role of the familiar in a witch's household was a general one. They acted as companions and assistants and were supposedly particularly useful in helping the witch to cause death and injury to her neighbours or their livestock or property. For example, familiars were meant to be able to cause milk to go sour, to make cows unable to give milk, to render animals sterile and to make crops fail. At the height of the witchcraft hysteria if an animal or bird, or even an insect, was spotted at the scene of death or disaster it was instantly identified as a familiar and a likely owner sought.

Owners of pets, particularly if they were old women who lived alone, were particularly at risk of being accused of keeping a familiar. When witchcraft hysteria was at its peak, however, and particularly during the ultra-zealous witch-finding activities, it was enough to be seen in the company of a creature, however accidental and brief this encounter was, to merit a charge of keeping a familiar.

A curious feature of the belief in familiars is that there are no records indicating that such creatures ever came to the aid of their accused owners. Mostly they seem to have disappeared. Sometimes a close watch was kept on imprisoned witches in case familiars adopted the shapes of insects and crept in to the prison to help their owners escape. It appears that they need not have bothered because the familiars seem to have turned out to be an ungrateful lot, despite the generous treatment that had been meted out to them by their owners.

Familiars are not unknown in modern witchcraft but these are not believed to be demons in disguise. Instead they are seen as animal companions that are often sensitive to psychic powers and vibrations.

goddess

In modern neo-pagan witchcraft it is the goddess, not the

devil, who is at the centre of its creed. She is regarded as being the source of magical power as well as being the major life force. Gerald Gardner did much to promote the importance of the goddess in modern witchcraft in the 1950s after the establishing of his own coven.

Modern witches have also been influenced by the feminist movement and the increased role of women in the world at large. This has added significantly to the emphasis that is laid on the role of the goddess in modern witchcraft.

In modern witchcraft there are often two beings at the head of the movement—the goddess and the horned god (page 215), a union of female and male. These are represented in covens by the high priestess and the high priest. On the other hand, there are some modern witches who regard only the goddess as the head of the movement. The goddess is frequently regarded as a trinity, known as the triple goddess, comprising the female roles of virgin, mother and crone.

goat

The goat is traditionally associated with virility and lust. In European witchcraft tradition, although rarely in England or Scotland, the goat was also frequently regarded as a shape adopted by the devil at orgiastic gatherings of witches, or sabbats. Several of the accused witches forced under torture to make supposedly voluntary confessions described the devil in the form of a goat presiding over rituals. Some also recounted how they had sexual intercourse with the devil in this shape or gave him an obscene kiss, a kiss on the buttocks.

In classical mythology the god Pan was depicted as a creature that was half-human, half-goat. A similar figure has been associated with witchcraft, although it is more associated with Satanism, the worship of the devil. The symbol of the satanic goat is known as Bahomet.

hare

The hare, like the cat, was associated with witchcraft on two counts. It was held to be a common familiar (page 210) of witches, using its famed ability for speed to help him or her carry out spells and harmful deeds. The hare was also thought to be a favourite shape adopted by witches as a disguise.

There are legends in which hunters wounded a hare only to see later an old hag in the village wounded in the same part of the body. Similar tales tell of hares being killed by hunters only to metamorphose back into human corpses.

Hecate

In Greek mythology, an ancient goddess whose powers were various. She could bestow wealth, victory and wisdom, good luck on sailors and hunters, prosperity on youth and on flocks. She was afterwards confused with other divinities and finally became especially an infernal goddess who was invoked by magicians and witches.

hedgehog

In common with the cat and the hare, the hedgehog was held to fulfil two roles in witchcraft. Although less commonly associated with witchcraft than the cat, the hedgehog was thought to be a favourite disguise of witches, able to infiltrate gardens, outhouses and even houses without attracting as much attention as a black cat or dog. So strong was this belief that many innocent hedgehogs were killed on the assumption that they might well be witches. The hedgehog was also thought to be an occasional familiar, particularly useful to witches who wished to do harm to livestock.

high priest *see* HORNED GOD; COVEN.

high priestess *see* GODDESS; COVEN.

horned god

In modern neo-pagan witchcraft the horned god is the male consort of the goddess. In covens he is represented by the high priest who sometimes wears a horned helmet or a headdress with antlers. Although the horned god in modern witchcraft is representative of sexuality, power and vitality, unlike the devil, he does not use his attributes in an evil way.

The concept of the horned god is thought to date back to Palaeolithic times. He was often depicted as being half-man and half-animal as well as wearing horns. He was traditionally associated with woodlands, the hunt and fertility.

horse

In pre-mechanical days the horse was extremely valuable to its owner, both as a form of transport and as a draught animal in agriculture. It was therefore seen as a prime target for the evil of witches who wished to bring harm to the owner. Owners feared that witches might make the horse go lame, become ill or even die. Because of this, horse-owners were wont to try to protect their animals from the spells of witches by surrounding them with things that were traditionally thought to ward off witches. They might hang a horseshoe on the stable door or hang a sprig of rowan on it. Alternatively, they might hang either on the stable door or round the animal's neck a stone with a hole in it, known as a hagstone and sometimes known as a witch-stone. It was thought that the hanging of brass bells or shining horse brasses on the horse would keep at bay any witches or familiars because they would be dazzled by the brightness of the objects.

Witches were alleged sometimes to borrow horses without permission in order to get to their orgiastic gatherings or sabbats. Supposedly, owners would be made aware of this unauthorised borrowing only in the morning, when the animals would be exhausted and sweating. Witches were also credited with the ability to stop a team of horses dead in their tracks and to keep them in that state until they chose to let them start up again. This could have a disastrous effect on farmers who were trying to plough fields, and some tried to avert this happening by having the driver of the said team of horses carry a whip made of rowan, a favourite anti-witch tree.

At the height of the witchcraft hysteria witches were alleged to adopt the shape of horses and thus probably saved themselves the bother of borrowing horses to transport them to their sabbats. The horse was also one of the shapes that the devil was thought to assume from time to time. The horse was regarded as being too big to be a familiar (page 210).

incubus

Incubus was the name given to a lustful demon that had sexual intercourse with women as they slept and made the women have erotic dreams. Such demons were thought to have associations with witchcraft in that they were alleged to have sexual intercourse with witches at sabbats, sometimes taking the forms of goats.

lizard

Lizards were thought to have at least two connections with witchcraft. The creature was widely believed to be a common ingredient in the renowned witch's brew of evil appearance and evil smell. It was also thought to be one of the shapes that a demon might adopt as a witch's familiar (page 210).

owl

The owl has had something of a mixed history in legend and mythology. To the ancient Greeks it was a symbol of wisdom, but the ancient Romans saw it as a bird of ill-omen whose presence or call often presaged death, illness or disaster. In the Middle Ages the owl was allegedly the shape sometimes adopted by a demon or familiar (page 210) when accompanying a witch on a broomstick or flying around helping her carry out her magic.

rabbit

Like the hare (page 214), the rabbit was traditionally held to be a possible disguise for a witch's familiar (page 210), which would hop around swiftly to aid her in carrying out her magic. As was also the case with the hare, the rabbit was held to be one of the common shapes that witches adopted to disguise themselves. It was bad luck for an old woman if she lived beside a field or wood containing rabbit warrens.

A rabbit's foot is traditionally associated with good luck.

raven

Because black has been traditionally associated with darkness and evil, black creatures throughout the ages have tended to be viewed with suspicion. Like the crow (page 206), but to an even greater extent, the raven was regarded as a bird of ill-omen whose presence was held to portend disaster or death. The raven was avoided as much as possible because it was a popular tradition that adopting the shape of a raven was a common pursuit of the devil.

At the time of the witchcraft hysteria it was alleged to be a favourite shape for a witch's familiar (page 210), having the ability to fly around the place helping her to carry out her black deeds against her neighbours. It was unfortunate for an old woman if she had a house near a place where ravens were liable to settle or gather, as this made her a prime target for accusations of witchcraft.

striga

The striga in classical mythology was a blood-drinking night-spirit. Striges were depicted as being women who could adopt the shape of terrible birds of prey with huge talons and mis-shapen heads. In such guises they were said to prey upon men and children as they lay asleep. They were alleged to have misshapen breasts full of poisonous milk that they fed to children. As far as men were concerned, the striges were alleged to turn back into women in the course of attacking them and had sexual intercourse with them.

As time went on the striges became identified with demonology, and in the Middle Ages they were regarded as female witches.

spider

The spider was associated with witchcraft in that it was alleged that witches used spiders, caught in pots, to cast spells in their practise of storm-raising. Otherwise spiders were regarded in many cultures as symbols of luck and considered to have the ability to ward off disease. It was considered unlucky to kill them.

toad

The toad is one of the creatures most commonly associated with witchcraft, and it was alleged to have several functions. It was said to act as a witch's familiar (page 210) to aid her in her acts of witchcraft, especially acts that involved the use of poison, and to accompany her to sabbats. Toads were quite common, and it was not necessary for a woman actually to possess one in order to be accused of having one as a familiar. A toad in the garden or anywhere near the house was enough to bring on the accusation. The creatures were regarded as having attributes that made them particularly suitable to be familiars in that they were allegedly easy to tame, easy to look after and were endowed with psychic powers.

The toad was also involved in shape-changing, which was a traditional feature of witchcraft. It was said to be a favourite shape for witches to adopt and it was thought that the devil himself sometimes changed into a toad.

The toad is traditionally associated with poison. Its skin contains glands that secrete a poisonous substance if the creature is alarmed in any way. This made the toad a favourite ingredient in witches' brews over which they cast their spells. Toads were also allegedly used by witches to make themselves invisible. In order to achieve this feat, witches are reputed to have mixed toad spittle and the sap of the sow thistle and then smeared the resultant potion on the skin in the shape of a crooked cross.

The toad was also supposedly useful in detecting poison as well as creating it. It was thought to carry a jewel inside its head that would become hot in the presence of poison. Such a stone was much sought after by people with enemies, and there were many stones that laid claim to be genuine toadstones but that were in fact fakes. A test of genuineness involved placing the stone in front of a toad. If the toad jumped towards the stone as if to take it, then the stone was held to be genuine.

Yet another association between witchcraft and the toad existed. Some witches were alleged to use them in a bizarre way to bring painful death to their enemies. Supposedly they avenging witches baptised toads with the names of the relevant enemies and then tortured the creatures to death under the belief that such action would bring a similar fate to the enemies.

Because of its associations with poison and witchcraft, and because it is regarded as an ugly creature, the toad has long been regarded with dislike or fear. Its reputation was not enhanced by the fact that it was thought to cause warts in anyone who handled it. On the other hand, people were reluctant to kill them, because tradition had it that killing a toad would bring on a storm of rain.

weasel

The weasel was held to be one of the animal shapes favoured by witches as disguise. This was perhaps because it is a swift, lithe animal that could slip in and out without being easily seen. As well as being associated with witchcraft, the weasel was thought to be a creature of ill-omen, bringing death or disaster by its presence or call. If one was unlucky enough to encounter or hear its call then the recommended way of supposedly warding off any ill effects was to throw three small stones or pebbles in front of one and to make the sign of the cross a total of seven times.

It was claimed that the gift of divination or prophesying would be granted to someone for a period of a year if he or she would only consume the heart of weasel while it was still beating.

wolf and werewolf

The wolf is traditionally regarded as a fierce, dangerous creature and associated with evil and the supernatural. In some European cultures the wolf was regarded as a creature of ill-omen whose appearance presaged death or disaster, and in some it was closely associated with the devil, being regarded as a favourite shape for the devil to adopt.

The wolf was also associated with witchcraft, especially at the height of witchcraft hysteria. Witches were popularly held in some areas to be able to turn themselves into wolves so that they could roam the land striking terror into people's hearts and inflicting injury and destruction. This alleged taking on of the shape of a wolf was known as lycanthropy.

When the accused witch allegedly took on the guise of a wolf, he or she was known as a werewolf, literally man-wolf, but, according to legend, there were other werewolves who were not witches. These were people who supposedly did not choose to adopt the shape of wolves but had been destined to do so, perhaps because they had been born under a curse. Such people, mostly but not always men, supposedly changed into wolves regularly, usually on nights of a full moon, and immediately took over the alleged attributes of wolves, fierceness and evil, whatever their attributes were when they were in their own shapes. Alleged signs of being a werewolf included having hair on the palms of the hands.

People

cowan

In modern neo-pagan witchcraft cowan is the term used for someone who is not a witch and so has not been initiated into witchcraft. The word is derived from a Scots word for a mason who did not serve an apprenticeship.

warlock

Warlock is a term sometimes used to describe a male witch or sorcerer. In modern witchcraft most men preferred to be known simply as witches and even historically the word witch was recognised as referring to either sex. In fact a huge proportion of accused witches were women.

white witch

White witch was the name given to someone who appeared to be endowed with magical powers but who used them for good rather than evil, black being the colour associated with those alleged witches who used their supposed gifts to cause harm. White witches, for example, might be herbalists and healers, but some were allegedly able to counteract evil spells, tell the future or mix love potions.

Unfortunately for many so-called white witches, to the investigators during the height of the witch hysteria it mattered not what the accused witch used her powers for. They regarded these as having come from the devil and so the white witch was as doomed as any other witch.

Plants

angelica

One of several plants traditionally thought to endow protection against witchcraft. It was also thought to protect against some diseases, such as the plague. This aromatic plant is sometimes called the Root of the Holy Ghost from its association with St Michael.

apple

The apple has long been associated with magic. Both the whole fruit and its peel were widely used in divination. In divination where there was a love interest it was thought that apple peel might take the form of the initial of a future love.

Witches were popularly thought to use apples in order to poison people, and this belief is reflected in the tale of Snow White, who was given a poisoned apple by her wicked stepmother that put her to sleep. Apples were also said to play a role in demonic possession since witches supposedly used the fruit to transmit the demon to the victim.

bay

The bay tree was often planted close to houses with a view to protecting its inhabitants. It was meant to be able to ward off disease, particularly the plague, as well as evil spirits and witches. The leaves of the tree were used as a means of prophesying the future. They were set alight and if they crackled as they burnt then all would be well. If, on the other hand, they burnt without making a noise then misfortune would occur. Bay leaves were also used medicinally by those who used plants in the treatment of various diseases and who were often suspected of witchcraft for so doing.

bryony

A climbing plant that is said to have acted as a substitute for mandrake in witches' potions and brews if they were unable to obtain the latter. Known for its aphrodisiac properties, bryony was also thought to increase fertility and was used in healing to reduce bruising.

deadly nightshade

This was used both as an aid to witchcraft and to ward it off. Witches were said to be able to increase their powers of divination if they consumed small amounts of the plant, the berries of which contain belladonna. If they overdid the dose, however, they could end up either dead or mad. The plant was also held to be one of the ingredients in the preparation known as flying ointment, traditionally concocted by witches to help them fly through the air.

If the plant was useful to witches, they also had cause to dislike and fear it. It was thought that a sprig of the plant either placed in a house or worn by a person had the property of warding off evil spirits, including witches, from livestock as well as people. Like other anti-evil plants, it was also thought to protect against disease.

egg tree

The egg tree was used in America to ward off witches and their magic. It was a dead bush that had its branches cropped and was then covered in a great many blown eggs and set up near a house or cabin.

elder

The elder was associated with witchcraft in that it was a favourite wood from which to fashion their wands. It was also said to be a common ingredient in witches' brews, the stems of the dwarf bush being a reddish colour in autumn and thought to look as though they contained blood. Elder trees were viewed with suspicion because they were thought to be inhabited by evil spirits and it was feared that the devil might come down the chimney if elder wood was burnt on the fire. Witches were supposed to have the ability to turn themselves into elder trees and were thought often to congregate under elder trees. There was a great fear of elder being brought indoors as it was thought that it would bring death into the house.

In common with deadly nightshade, however, the elder tree was considered to have anti-evil properties as well as evil ones. Cutting a stem from a dwarf elder bush was regarded as being a way of causing injury to any nearby witch. Furthermore, the elder could be used to identify witches and ward off any injurious actions that they might be plotting. This was supposedly done by smearing a little elder juice on the eyes, an action that was meant to result in the person so treated being able to see any witches who were in the neighbourhood and to perceive what they were up to.

Although elder was not to be taken indoors, it was regarded as being a good thing to hang a bough of it, cut on the last day of April, at the entrance to the house since this acted as a deterrent to witches and warded off their magic. Amulets of elder worn by people were meant to have the same effect.

fern

The fern was one of several plants that were associated with both witchcraft and anti-witchcraft activity. Seeds collected from the plant on Midsummer's Eve and carried around were thought to enable the carrier to become invisible. Such seeds were also thought to be an ingredient in flying ointment, a preparation allegedly made by witches to enable them to fly through the air.

An anti-witchcraft device could be made from the male fern if was gathered on Midsummer Eve's and the fronds removed until there were only five remaining, leaving the plant resembling the human hand. This was then smoked over a bonfire until it became hard. It was then thought to be ready to confer immunity from the evil of witches or evil spirits on the person who carried it. Because of its resemblance to the human hand it was known as a lucky hand.

foxglove

Originally known as folk's glove, but also known as witches' glove, the plant was thought to be poisonous and a common ingredient in witches' potions. Many people who were accused of witchcraft in England and Scotland were simply people who experimented with herbs to try to alleviate or cure injuries or disease.

The foxglove was one of the plants used by such people, and in the middle of the eighteenth century a Shropshire doctor, William Withering, discovered that the foxglove did indeed have curative properties. Having heard of the success of a supposed witch in curing dropsy, he contacted her, learned of her use of foxglove and extracted from it the unknown drug now known as digitalis. This discovery proved to be a major breakthrough in the treatment of heart disease and the drug was later synthesised.

garlic

Traditionally garlic was known for its healing and beneficial properties and indeed has become so again nowadays when there has been a renaissance in herbal medicine. It is used, for example, as an aid to the cure and prevention of colds and other infections. The ancient Romans gave it to soldiers to wear in battle in the belief that it would raise their courage levels.

However, garlic was also used traditionally as a powerful protective agent against the forces of evil. Witches, demons and vampires were all thought to be deterred by this pungent plant. Garlands of garlic were worn around the neck or hung in houses, often near windows, with such a purpose in mind. Garlic collected in the month of May was thought to be particularly effective. The Greek hero Odysseus is said to have used garlic to protect his men against the witchcraft of Circe, the sorceress who had the ability to turn people into swine.

Garlic was also used in informal trials. Someone suspected

of a crime was asked to throw a clove of garlic into a fire. If the clove popped the person was considered to be guilty.

hawthorn

Hawthorn is one of several trees and plants that were credited with being used both by witches and against them. The tree was long thought to be cursed because thorns from it were thought to have formed the crown that was put on Christ's head when he was being crucified.

Witches were thought to use thorns from the hawthorn when they were jabbing effigies so as to cause pain, injury or death to the person whom the effigy represented. The thorns were also thought to feature in other black magic practices.

The hawthorn was, however, also used as a witch deterrent. A hawthorn bush planted by a house entrance was thought to ward off witches, it being thought that they might get caught in the thorns.

People seem to have been slightly ambivalent about hawthorn blossom. On one hand, it was considered to be unlucky to take hawthorn blossom indoors. On the other hand, some thought that decorating the rooms of a house with hawthorn blossom would keep witches and other evil spirits at bay.

hazel

The hazel tree was one of several trees and plants that was thought to be both advantageous and disadvantageous to witches. The wood was so prized by witches for its magical properties that they used it to make their wands. The nuts were used at Hallowe'en in a procedure that was intended to check up on the fidelity of a lover. Two nuts were placed in the fire by the person testing a lover's fidelity. If the lover was un-faithful the nuts would jump in the air.

Hazel was also used to protect against witchcraft. Sprigs of witch hazel would be tied over the entrance to houses to stop witches from going in and to ward off their magic.

hemlock

Hemlock, being a poisonous plant, was traditionally associated with the devil and with witches. It was credited with the ability to summon demons and was supposedly much used in witches' brews and potions. Hemlock was held to be one of several ingredients that went into the preparation of flying ointment with which witches allegedly smeared themselves to help them in the process of flying through the air.

henbane

Henbane is a poisonous plant and so was a natural plant to be associated with witchcraft. Witches were meant to use it in their brews over which they concocted their spells. When the plant was burnt the fumes were said to conjure up demons. The plant was also said to be a useful aid to clairvoyance, and it was used in love potions because of its supposed aphrodisiac properties.

mandrake

Mandrake is a poisonous plant that grows in the Mediterranean region. Traditionally a major ingredient of witches' brews, the root of the plant was thought to have valuable magical properties as well as being considered to be an effective soporific and aphrodisiac. The thick root of the plant is meant to resemble a human in shape – hence its name, and it was used traditionally in healing as well as a magic ingredient.

It was believed in medieval times that witches harvested their mandrake roots from the bottom of gallows trees. This was because the mandrake plant was supposed to spring up from the semen or other body droppings that fell from the decomposing corpses of those who had committed crimes and had been executed for these.

Skill was thought to be required in digging up the root of the mandrake. Digging it up with one's own hands was meant to end in agonising death or impotence. It was thought safer to use a dog in the plant's uprooting. According to one tradition, it was enough simply to get a dog to dig up the root, but according to another the procedure of uprooting involved digging around all but a very small portion of the root. A dog was then tied to this and left. On trying to follow its owner the dog would pull out the root, often strangling itself in the process. As the root parted company with the soil, it was alleged to let out a loud, terrifying shriek and sometimes to sweat blood.

It was said that witches sometimes undertook a spell to endow the mandrake root with the gift of speech, having first covered it in human blood and placed berries on it to represent eyes and mouth. If the spell worked, the mandrake root was then said to be able to communicate to witches information about what was going to happen in the future and also to advise them of the location of hidden treasure.

marigold

The marigold flowers were much used in herbal healing. For example, if it was rubbed on the skin it was thought to reduce inflammation and swelling from bites, stings and injuries. The flowers were also thought to be an aphrodisiac and so were used in love potions.

However, the marigold had a specific use in witchcraft in that it was considered to be a witch deterrent. It was often therefore planted near the entrance to a house to prevent witches from entering. Its flowers were also taken inside to ward off the evil and magic of witches.

mistletoe

Mistletoe is an evergreen shrub that from early times has been associated with the occult, having been associated with the Celtic druids who considered it sacred, like the oak tree on which it often grew. It has been used in various ways as a healing agent but it was also used as protection against witchcraft, ill-fortune and disease. It was thus hung in homes, barns and stables. A sprig of mistletoe hung from a doorway was thought to deter witches from entering the building.

mountain ash *see* ROWAN TREE.

mugwort

This plant was traditionally considered to be an effective witch deterrent. It was also thought that it could act as an antidote against several poisons and that it could be used to undo the effects of spells. The plant was also thought to protect against the plague and other diseases and to counteract the effects of fatigue

oak

The oak tree was sacred in Celtic lore and has traditionally been regarded as providing protection against evil and witchcraft. Sprigs of the tree were hung in houses or worn by people as a witch deterrent, and standing under an oak tree was thought to serve the same purpose. Trees planted at the entrance to buildings were believed to prevent witches from entering, and when the trees were planted at a crossroads their anti-evil properties were thought to be particularly effective.

oak apple

A gall formed on an oak tree, caused by a kind of wasp larva, is sometimes called an oak apple. Oak apples were traditionally used to ascertain whether or not a young child had been bewitched. For this purpose three oak apples were cut from a tree and dropped into a vessel of water. The vessel was then placed under the child's cradle amid strict silence. If the oak apples floated to the top of the water the child was deemed to be safe but if they sank to the bottom then it was deemed certain that the child had been placed under a witch's spell.

pumpkin

The pumpkin is much used to form lanterns in the festivities surrounding the American custom known as trick or treat. This takes place on Hallowe'en, and the pumpkin is now becoming increasingly commonly used for lanterns in Britain, even Scotland, where the traditional Hallowe'en lantern is made out of a turnip, a much harder vegetable to hollow out than the pumpkin.

The pumpkin is one of several plants and trees that were traditionally held to provide protection against evil in general. In order to maximise this property of the plant, it was considered best to plant them on Good Friday.

rosemary

Rosemary was associated with witchcraft in that it was thought to be able to ward off the harmful effects of the evil eye by which a person was bewitched if a witch cast a baleful glare at him or her. Sprigs of rosemary were worn by people on their persons or hung on the front door of a house to prevent witches working their magic. The plant was also regarded as being a useful aid to divination.

rowan

The rowan tree, also known as the mountain ash, was traditionally held to be a powerful protector against the power of witches. Trees were often planted in gardens or near the entrance to buildings to ensure that witches did not cross the threshold, and even the dead were protected from the evil of witchcraft by planting rowan trees in churchyards. People sometimes wore sprigs of rowan in their hats and sprigs were tied to bedsteads. Boughs of it were sometimes hung in barns, stables and cow sheds to protect livestock from witchcraft. Sometimes farm animals had twigs of rowan attached to their tails to prevent interference from witches.

The wood was sometimes used to make riding whips as a witch deterrent, and piles of it were sometimes kept inside a house with the same purpose. When new houses were being built, rowan was sometimes used in parts of their structure to keep the inhabitants witchcraft-free.

So powerful an anti-witch agent was rowan considered to be that a witch touched by a rowan branch was supposedly instantly to be taken off by the devil to Hell.

stonecrop

Stonecrop is a flowering plant the habitat of which is rocks or walls. It was often grown by doorways in the belief that it would prevent witches from entering, and sprigs of it were taken into houses for the same purpose

willow

Willow was traditionally much used in herbal medicine because of its alleged curative properties. Some varieties were used as a protection against witchcraft, although witches were alleged often to use it for making wands. It was a popular tradition that it was unlucky to bring willow catkins into a house or to burn willow wood on a fire indoors

witch hazel *see* HAZEL.

wych elm

Also known as witch elm, this tree was meant to impart luck to anyone who carried a twig of it and also to protect the carrier from witchcraft.

yarrow

Yarrow is one of several plants that were thought to deter witches and their evil doings. Consequently sprigs of it were worn on the person or taken into houses.

It was used in divination when this related to a vision of someone's future lover, the person seeking such a vision being advised to sleep with a sprig under his or her pillow.

yew

With reference to witchcraft the yew tree was considered to provide protection against witchcraft. It was also thought to protect people from ghosts and evil in general and was often planted in churchyards.

On the other hand, witches were said sometimes to use it to make wands. Some traditions indicate that it was considered unlucky to take yew into a house or to cut down a yew tree as this would bring ill-luck

Substances

amber

Amber, which is yellowish fossilized resin, was traditionally considered to protect against witchcraft or other evil. It was used in jewellery or in amulets for this purpose and to bring good luck to the wearer. Amber was also considered to have curative properties in the case of certain illnesses.

blood

Blood, which was considered to represent a person's life-force, was associated with witchcraft in various ways. Witches could get power over their enemies or over people whom they wished to harm by getting hold of a few drops of their blood. They could then make use of it in the weaving of their harmful spells and are alleged to have put samples of the blood into harmful brews or potions or else to have incorporated the blood in effigies, doll-like representations of the people whom they intended to harm.

Blood has long had associations with the making of pacts. Sometimes people cut their wrists so that their blood could mingle, this being a method of making an agreement that was totally binding. Another unbreakable pact could be achieved by signing the said pact in blood. Thus it was that the pact which witches were supposed to make with the devil as a sign of their allegiance to him was supposedly signed by them in their blood. This devil's pact was a common feature in witches' confessions, but this was because the questions put to witches to get them to confess were of such a standard nature that the confessions were bound to be similar.

The keeping of familiars (page 210) by witches allegedly often involved blood. Witches were widely believed to reward these creatures for their good work by treating them to a few drops of their own blood, sucked from their fingers, protuberances on their skin or occasionally from supernumerary nipples. Such blood marks were zealously searched for during investigations following charges of witchcraft.

Because a person's blood was meant to contain his or her life-force, it was thought that the magical powers of a witch resided in the blood. It was also thought that this power could be transmitted from generation to generation and that such power could be destroyed only by destroying a witch's blood. Thus it was that, although in England witches tended to be executed by hanging, on mainland Europe, and sometimes in Scotland, witches were routinely burnt at the stake. By burning the witches to ashes the authorities believed that they could destroy a witch's blood and her power, although as an act of great clemency convicted witches were often allowed to be strangled first, provided they had confessed.

Blood was also used in attempts at breaking the power of witches when they were still alive. In the common practice of scoring above the breath, suspected witches were attacked and cut somewhere above their mouths or noses. It was believed that if they bled from such areas then they would lose their magical powers.

In another measure believed to neutralise the power of a witch, a witch bottle was prepared. This contained some blood taken from a victim of witchcraft as well as samples of hair, nails and urine. These were then boiled together at midnight, causing much agony in the witch who had bewitched the victim and nullifying her magic. Alternatively the bottle was buried with the same result. Sometimes it was said that the witch bottle could result in the death of a witch.

bloodstone

A variety of semiprecious stone, bloodstone was much used in healing but it was also thought to be endowed with magical properties. It was thought to be an aid to the divination of natural disasters, such as storms and floods. Bloodstone was also thought to protect against evil, including witchcraft, but it was also used by witches in their magic, being thought to have the property of granting wishes.

brass

Brass was traditionally considered to be a substance that could protect against witchcraft and other forms of evil. Thus it was used in the making of amulets, worn by people to protect their persons from evil or ill-luck, and it was also used to hang on horses, in the form of horse brasses or bells, or on cows, in the form of bells to protect the livestock from the machinations of witches.

hair

Human hair was thought to be connected with witchcraft in several ways. The hair was thought to retain a strong connection with the person from whom it had been taken. This therefore meant that a witch was in a position to do more harm to an intended victim if she had some of his or her hair, even a strand or two, when putting together spells. It was also thought that people who were thought to be likely victims of witchcraft were advised to bury, or otherwise get rid of, any of their hair that was cut off to prevent a witch from getting hold of it.

It was thought that a witch could cause terrible pain to an intended victim simply by throwing a strand of his or her hair in the fire. The making of effigies, or wax images, was a favourite way for witches to harm people of their choice. If some of the relevant person's hair was incorporated into such an effigy the magic was alleged to be more powerful.

Hair was often used in the contents of a witch bottle, which was a bottle or flask filled with various ingredients, including urine and nail clippings, taken from someone who was suspected of being bewitched, the bottle being then buried or heated on a fire. The purpose of this was to counteract any spells that might have been cast by causing pain to the bewitcher. If the bottle exploded this was meant to signal the death of the witch.

Strength and power were thought in early times to reside in

the hair. For example, in the biblical story Samson was deprived of his strength when Delilah cut off his hair. It was thus believed that at least some of the magical powers of witches resided in their hair. If a witch shook her head it was thought by this act of shaking her hair that she had doubled her power in strength.

When witches were arrested they were often shorn of their hair. This was partly as an act of humiliation or degradation but it was also seen as a means of depriving them of their power. Hair-shaving was also carried out to get rid of any demons or familiars that might be lurking there with a view to helping the accused witches. Another reason for the cutting of the hair of the accused witches was to allow the investigators to search particularly thoroughly for signs of the devil's mark, a mark made by the devil on a witch when he or she swore allegiance to him.

holy water *see* WATER.

iron

Although iron was traditionally used by witches, in that their cauldrons and many of their utensils were made of it, the metal was long held in folklore in many parts of the world to be a protector against evil spirits. It was commonly used to make amulets to give protection against evil, danger or ill-luck. With specific reference to witchcraft, it was believed in Europe that witches were unable to cross cold iron. With this tradition in mind, people were advised to bury a knife beneath the doorsteps of their houses so that witches would not dare to enter.

lead

According to some traditions, lead might be used in tests undertaken to determine whether or not there was witchcraft afoot. One test involved the dropping of a piece of molten lead into a vessel of water and waiting to see if the piece of lead solidified into a shape discernibly resembling something. If the piece of metal did take on a discernible shape then there was indeed witchcraft in the air and the person who was believed to be the victim of this was urged to wear the said piece of lead over his or her heart as a protection against harm by witchcraft.

Caskets containing religious relics and coffins containing corpses were formerly made of lead partly to keep away evil spirits.

nail clippings

It was thought that witches would be able to make exceptionally effective spells against someone if they had possession of something that had been part of his or her body. Thus, as was also the case with hair, a witch in possession of nail clippings could do a great deal of harm to the person from whose nails they came. It was, therefore, thought advisable for people to bury nail clippings in order to prevent a witch getting hold of these.

Nail clippings were also sometimes used along with hair (page 238) and urine in the creation of a witch bottle, which was used to counteract the effects of any evil spells that had been cast.

poison

Poison was traditionally associated with the practice of witchcraft. During the witchcraft hysteria, many people were accused of being witches because they had killed people by means of poison or made them ill by it. Before the days of specific tests it was often difficult to disprove this, especially if, as was not infrequently the case, the accused was someone who used herbs and plants to help heal people. It was thought that such people might just be using their supposed healing powers as a front while they used their knowledge of plants to poison people.

It was popularly assumed that the traditional witches' brew contained poisons. These were thought to include such poisonous plants as deadly nightshade but also poison taken from the toad.

salt

Traditionally salt was held to be anathema to evil creatures of all kinds. Its very function as a preservative made it an opposing force to the corruption of witchcraft, demons, etc. In addition it was used in Christianity to consecrate churches, and salted holy water was used in baptism. Thus salt was thought to be a deterrent to witches and their evil ways.

Witches were popularly held to be unable to eat anything salted. Salt was meant to be absolutely excluded from any of the feasts at the orgiastic sabbats, and when pressure was being applied to suspected witches to get them to confess they were sometimes force-fed extremely salty food. This was supposedly in order that they would refuse the food and confess but actually it was a form of torture in that the accused witches were force-fed such food and then deprived of water after they had developed a raging thirst.

Salt was used in various ways as a protective against witchcraft. Newborn babies might be bathed in salted water or made to eat a little salt to protect them against the evil of witchcraft. Dairymaids would sometimes put a little salt into their milk pails or butter churns so that witches would not turn the milk sour or the butter rancid.

It was thought that salt could also be used as a means of dispelling the power of a witch, even when this had taken hold. Spells were supposedly able to be broken by the action of throwing a handful of salt into the household fire every morning for nine consecutive days. Another tradition suggested that one way to break a witch's spell involved the stealing of a tile from the roof of her house. This was then to be sprinkled with a mixture of salt and urine and heated over the fire.

If a person was so unlucky as to have a witch curse him or her, it was thought that such a curse could be negated by the throwing of a handful of salt after the retreating witch. It was fortunate in such cases that some people did carry salt around with them as a deterrent against witchcraft.

spittle

Spittle was thought to have various connections with witchcraft. It was thought, for instance, that witches used their own spittle while effecting curses or harmful spells against someone. The spittle of an intended victim was also thought to be useful to witches in that it was thought to increase the power of a spell against him or her. It was thus considered unwise to spit indiscriminately.

Witches had another connection with spittle. It was believed that witches were unable to shed tears. Aware of this, the interrogators of accused witches on mainland Europe in the Middle Ages and the Renaissance accused them of having smeared spittle on their faces to emulate tears if they were found to have wet cheeks.

Spittle was thought to play a protective role in cases of the evil eye. If a witch looked at someone with a particularly baleful expression, it was thought that she was fixing him or her with the evil eye or overlooking them. By such means did she bewitch them. Spittle was thought to be able to help in reversing such bewitchment. It was thought that this might be brought about by spitting in the witch's eye.

urine

Urine was thought to have various connections with witchcraft. If a witch got hold of some of an intended victim's urine then this, like the possession of hair, nail clippings, and spittle, gave the witch more power over her victim and made her evil spell more potent. In order to prevent the witch getting hold of urine and using it for harmful purposes, likely victims were urged to spoil it in some way, for example by washing the hands in it, so that it would be rendered unsuitable for use in spells.

If a spell was put on someone then one possible counteraction involved getting hold of some of the witch's urine. This was then bottled and buried, or sometimes boiled. Such actions had the effect of making the witch ill, and often unable to urinate, and sometimes of killing her. Alternatively, a cake could be made of ingredients that included some of the bewitched's party, and perhaps some nail clippings. The cake was then tossed in a fire. Still another method of breaking a spell that involved urine was in the making of a witch bottle. This was a flask or bottle filled with such ingredients as the urine, hair and nail clippings of the victim of a witch's spells and either buried, boiled on a fire or thrown on a fire.

Urine was also said to be a useful witch-deterrent. It was suggested that families wishing to keep witches out of their houses should sprinkle the doorposts with urine. An even more drastic measure involved sprinkling the members of the family with urine.

It was alleged that at the orgiastic gatherings of witches, known as sabbats, and at black masses (page 283) blasphemous travesties of religious ceremonies were held at which urine was substituted for holy water.

water

It was a widely held belief that witches or evil spirits could not cross water. There are several tales about people saving themselves from the clutches of witches or demons by jumping over stretches of water or crossing bridges. One of the most famous of these concerns the character Tam o' Shanter in the poem of the same name by Robert Burns. After a particularly drunken session with his friends, Tam was riding home pursued by a young witch whom he had spied on dancing in a churchyard. He narrowly escaped being caught by her by riding over a river.

Water that had been consecrated in a religious ritual was anathema to witches and other evil spirits. Holy water that had been used at services conducted during Easter was thought to be a particularly powerful deterrent against witches and demons. As a witch-deterrent, holy water was sprinkled on houses, farm animals and crops to prevent interference from witches. In many places there was a man who went around delivering holy water for such purposes. Those taking part in witchcraft trials as investigators, torturers, juries or judges were often advised to keep a dish of holy water so that they might use it to ward off any manifestations of witchcraft. In the well-known film *The Wizard of Oz*, the character called the Wicked Witch of the West simply melts away when covered in water.

Water was involved in a notorious test of witchcraft. This was known as swimming (*see* Chapter 2, Witchcraft Trials and Executions, page 77). In the carrying out of the test an accused witch was bound hand and foot and thrown into a stretch of water. If he or she sank it was seen as proof of innocence, although the exercise often resulted in death. If, on the other hand, he or she floated to the surface then this was taken as a sign of guilt. It was sometimes held that the water would not accept someone who had turned his or her back on Christianity and baptism and become a heretic.

Water was used in various healing processes. In neo-pagan witchcraft salted water is used to purify tools and to anoint participants in the rites.

Objects, Places and Concepts

aiguillette

Witches were alleged to use this knotted loop of thread to induce dissatisfaction in marriage, particularly to induce impotence, or even castration, in men and sterility in women. The device was also thought to incite couples to enter into adulterous relationships. The idea was particularly popular in France in the sixteenth century, and people were so convinced by its validity that many couples got married secretly and privately rather than publicly in church where the witch might get to work with her aiguillette during the marriage ceremony.

amulet

The concept of an amulet, an object that would protect against harm, goes back to earliest times and survives to modern times. The word comes from the Latin *amuletum*, meaning 'means of defence'. Amulets were typically worn on the body, often being worn round the neck, but this was not necessarily the case.

Amulets were widely used outside witchcraft for their supposed healing properties. However, they were specifically used to protect against witchcraft when witchcraft hysteria was its height. They sometimes took the form of pieces of paper on which were written some kind of holy words, such as the Lords' Prayer, in the hope that witches would be deterred from practising their craft by the presence of something associated with God.

bell

The ringing of church bells was considered to be anathema to witches and evil spirits, and they quickly disappeared at the first sound of them. During times such as Hallowe'en when witches held their sabbats, or orgiastic gatherings, townspeople would ring the church bells so that the witches would not fly over their houses on their way to the gathering. So powerful were church bells as a witch-deterrent that witches were said to fall off their broomsticks if they heard them ring. Storms were often assumed to be the result of a witch's deliberate storm-raising. Therefore, at the first signs of a storm, townspeople sometimes rang the church bells to dispel the evil work of the witch.

Other bells were also thought to be a witch-deterrent. Bells were sometimes hung at entrances to prevent witches and evil spirits from crossing the threshold. They were also frequently hung around the necks of horses, cows or other livestock to keep them safe from witchcraft, and human beings sometimes wore them as amulets.

According to some traditions, bells could sometimes be put to use by witches and sorcerers to summon the dead. It was thought that for bells to be used in this way they had to be made from a particular combination of metals, inscribed with various symbols. Tradition had it that the bell was then wrapped in green cloth and buried in the middle of a grave in a churchyard for seven days. The bell was then thought to be suitable for the purpose of summoning the dead.

black book *see* GRIMOIRE.

bodkin

Bodkins were frequently used in the test for witchcraft known as pricking (*see* Chapter 2, Witchcraft Trials and Executions, page 75). The sharp end of a bodkin would be used to prod an accused witch all over in an attempt to find a spot that was insensitive and so thought to be a mark of the devil. If the accused person was showing no sign of having such insensitive areas then the investigators would often use a cunning ploy. They would stab one area of the body with the sharp end of a bodkin exceptionally violently and then immediately touch another area of the same body very lightly with the blunt end. The result often was that the person concerned was hurt so badly by the sharp stabbing that he or she almost failed to notice the touch of the blunt end and so was put in the supposed position of having an insensitive area of the body, a supposed mark of the devil.

book of shadows

This was a kind of guidebook to witchcraft, being a book outlining beliefs, rituals, chants, dances, spells, etc. There was no universal book of shadows for witchcraft in general. Each tradition, and even each coven, might have its own adaptations and variations. Such books are a major part of modern witchcraft, but little is known about their role in early times. There is some suggestion that spells, etc, were recorded informally and secretly in books, but witchcraft, until relatively late on, seems to have been largely an oral tradition. It may have been more of a written tradition than was generally assumed since it appears to have been traditional for a witch's book of shadows to be destroyed when she died.

However, Gerald Gardner (*see* Chapter 3, Witches and Magicians: The Accused and Self-Confessed, page 132), who is regarded as being the father of modern witchcraft, came into possession of the fragments of such a book when he was initiated into a coven of hereditary witches in 1939, but this was greatly amplified and changed by him and his assistant, Doreen Valiente, some of the non-traditional material coming from the works of Aleister Crowley. This Gardnerian book of shadows was in turn adapted by Alexander Sanders, and his work has consequently inspired other books in other traditions.

broomstick

When we think of witches we think of broomsticks. They are an essential part of the witchcraft tradition as evinced in fairy tales and have become part of the cultural stereotype of the witch. Witches were alleged to use broomsticks to transport them to coven meetings and sabbats. They also supposedly used them to fly out to sea in order to indulge in storm-raising (page 280).

Since the fifteenth century the broomstick was associated with witches as a means of transport through the air, although it was not the only means of air transport associated with witchcraft. Up until the late sixteenth century other implements, such as forks, shovels or cleft sticks, were associated with witch travel. It was also alleged that some witches used their familiars to transport them through the air to coven meetings and sabbats.

The creature most often suspected of being a witch's familiar was the cat, and so this was the creature that was most frequently thought to carry a witch through the air. According to one theory, the reason the broomstick is associated with witches can be put down to a linguistic misunderstanding involving the word 'cat'. This theory suggests that 'cat' is an old dialect word for broomstick and that it was originally not the broomstick but the animal that was connected with witch travel.

The most usual reason given for the broomstick being involved in witch travel is that the broom was regarded as a symbol of woman, since it represented her domestic role in the home. Most accused witches were women. Witches were alleged to fly up the chimney on their broomsticks prior to setting off on their journeys. This belief is thought to be based on the fact that many women were in the habit of propping their brooms by the chimney or pushing it partly up the chimney to indicate her absence from home.

Yet another theory suggests that the witches' use of the broomstick as a medium of travel is a throwback to pagan times. In order to try to make their crops grow higher, it is said that people then used to mount poles, broomsticks, pitchforks, etc, and ride them like hobbyhorses through the fields, leaping as high as they could.

Although broomsticks are now very much associated with the legends of witchcraft in medieval times and in the Renaissance time, the connection between witch travel and broomsticks was much more common in continental Europe than in England. Brooms were rarely mentioned in witchcraft trials, and English witchcraft laws did not refer specifically to flying.

Witches were alleged to smear either themselves or their brooms with a preparation known as flying ointment (page 260), which they made specially with a view to improving their flying ability. It was alleged by some that the devil gave each witch a broomstick and some flying ointment on the occasion of her initiation. Others claimed that such gifts were given only to those who were weak and infirm and that it was only witches in the latter category who used broomsticks to transport them to coven meetings and sabbats.

At first witches were depicted as flying with the business end of the broom, that made out of twigs, pointing downwards, it being suggested that by this means were the witches' tracks swept away. It this image of the flying witch that is popular today, but at the end of the seventeenth century witches were often depicted as riding broomsticks with the end containing the bundle of twigs pointing upwards, sometimes holding a candle to light the way on dark nights.

It was alleged that witches sometimes fell off their broomsticks. This supposedly happened when a novice witch was unskilled in the art of travel by broomstick. Alternatively, it was alleged to happen if the townspeople rang the church bells as witches were flying over their town on known witch festival nights such as Hallowe'en. Townspeople were alleged to lay scythes and cutting hooks on the ground in order to kill any falling witches.

The broom is sometimes used in modern witchcraft as one of the witches' tools. It is used, for example, to sweep away evil or bad fortune.

cakes and wine

In modern witchcraft an esbat (*see* COVEN, page 283) usually ends with the partaking of cakes and wine, or sometimes beer or fruit juice, as an act of thanksgiving. The refreshments are often blessed by the high priest and high priestess and a thanksgiving offering made to the deities.

Cakes and wine were also thought to be served at some sabbats.

candle

Candles were alleged to have been associated with witchcraft in several ways. Traditionally they were used at sabbats in rites that were a travesty of Christian religious ceremonies. They were supposedly lit as a mark of loyalty to the devil, who supposedly often appeared at sabbats with a lighted candle placed between his horns. The witches supposedly lit their candles from this or else the devil lit them for them.

Candles made of human fat were allegedly used at black masses (page 283) in the seventeenth century. On a more mundane level, witches were sometimes supposed to put candles on their broomsticks to light their way on dark nights.

Witches were supposed also to use candles in their efforts to harm people. They allegedly identified a particular wax candle with a particular person and then, on the analogy of sticking pins into effigies or images of people, they stuck the candle with pins and set it alight, hoping to cause great pain or even death to the person with whom the candle had been identified.

Candles were thought to be able to dispel evil in some cases. If lit by the side of a dying person they were thought to have the ability to keep away demons or other evil things.

cauldron

Like the broomstick, the cauldron is an essential part of the archetypal witch according to modern perception. The cauldron played a major part in early Celtic culture, especially in the case of the Irish Celts. It was a symbol of abundance and was thought never to run out of food at a feast. It was also seen as a symbol of regeneration, an aspect of the cauldron that was revived by the modern witch Gerald Gardner (page 132) in a celebration of the winter solstice at which the cauldron was set alight. The coven then danced with increasing speed round it and the high priest and high priestess joined hands and leapt over the burning cauldron, followed by the other members of the coven.

It was popularly thought that a witch kept a cauldron on

the boil in order to weave evil spells. The cauldron was meant to contain an evil witches' brew containing such things as bat's blood, toads and their poison, lizards, various poisonous plants and even human flesh or fat. Over this brew the witch was meant to mutter incantations and cast spells to harm people or animals. Witches were thought to be able to cause storms at sea by throwing the contents of their cauldrons into the sea. They traditionally concocted their flying ointment (page 260) in their cauldrons.

The cauldron supposedly played an important part at sabbats, but this time its role was that of a cooking pot. The devil, or his representative, if he was not present, would preside over the cauldron that provided the feast of which all the witches partook. Individual witches allegedly took their cauldrons to sabbats where, it was said, they sometimes boiled up babies or small children for the sabbat feast.

charm wand

A charm wand was a glass stick, often formed like a walking stick, that was filled with tiny seeds or beads or else decorated with countless hairlines in the glass. It was kept in a house, and its supposed purpose was to prevent demons or other evil beings such as witches from carrying out any evil deeds. Apparently the belief was that evil beings would be diverted from their evil purposes by a desire to count the seed, beads or hairlines.

cross

It was widely believed that witches, demons and other evil beings were unable to withstand the power of the cross, the powerful Christian symbol. Thus people either wore crosses or made the sign of the cross to ward off the evil power of witches.

crossroads

The point where roads intersect has long been associated with magic and evil. Hecate, the Greek goddess of witchcraft, was also goddess of crossroads and animals were sacrificed to her there. Witches were alleged to gather at crossroads in order to conjure up the devil and his demons, and some spells were considered to be more effective if they were cast at a cross roads.

The evil reputation of crossroads was enhanced by the fact that it was often the site of the local gallows. The bodies of suicides, criminals and convicted vampires were often buried near a crossroads, supposedly because the ghost of the deceased would be unable decide which road take to get back home.

devil's mark

This was a mark supposedly put by the devil on initiates to witchcraft. This mark was allegedly made in several ways. The devil might simply touch the skin of the initiates with his finger, place a kiss on it, rake it with his claw or brand it with a hot iron. Such marks if found on the body of an accused witch were taken as proof positive of involvement with witchcraft.

The marks were routinely searched for during the investigation of an accused witch. The search was often extremely humiliating to the people involved, usually women. The devil supposedly often chose to leave his mark on a place on the body where it was most likely to remain hidden, under the eyelids, under the armpits, in the genitalia area or body cavities. Fortunately for the investigators, the exact nature of a devil's mark was ill-defined. Some such marks might be of a particular shape, such as cloven hoof, a hare, a spider or other creature. It is extremely easy to imagine that marks bear a resemblance to something and, in any case, the shape was not always held to be important.

Despite the nebulous nature of the alleged devil's mark, it was widely believed that it was extremely easy to differentiate between the devil's mark and other innocent marks on the skin. Given the circumstances, this would clearly not have been the case, especially where the investigator was intent on finding a devil's mark where at all possible. Nevertheless, this belief made the doctors who advised on the searches reluctant to raise the point that ordinary marks, such as birthmarks, looked much the same as supposed devil's marks.

The absence of an obvious mark did not save an accused witch, because it was alleged that sometimes the devil was so cunning as to leave an invisible mark. Patches of insensitive skin that did not bleed were thought to be particularly connected with the devil. In order to identify such areas of the body, accused witches were subject to the painful act of pricking (page 75). This involved being jabbed all over by a sharp object such as a bodkin (page 247).

The concept of a devil's mark seems to us now unbelievable, but many thousands of people, especially in continental Europe, were executed on the strength of this supposed backup evidence to the original, often baseless, accusation.

devil's pact

The devil's pact was a pact entered into by someone being initiated into witchcraft by the devil. This played a great part in many witchcraft trials and was mentioned in the *Malleus Maleficarum* (page 266), a guide to witchcraft and to the prosecution of accused witches. The concept of the devil's pact was enthusiastically embraced by the Inquisition, as this was held to show that witchcraft was simply an extension of heresy, witches being clearly seen to be turning to the devil and away from God. Getting accused witches to confess to having signed a pact with the devil was a major part of the investigation, and torturing of accused witches and references to this were an essential part of the standard catalogue of questions in investigations.

The pact with the devil could be an oral one, according to tradition, but more usually it was written down on a blank piece of parchment and signed in blood, the initiate being required to use blood taken from the left hand. The absence of such supposedly written documentation was put down to the fact that the devil usually kept the actual pacts, although a piece of paper purporting to be such a document was produced at the trial of Urbain Grandier in relation to the Loudun nuns (*see* Chapter 3, Witches and Magicians: The Accused and Self-Confessed, page 140).

Signing such a pact with the devil supposedly ensured the devil's help with the working of magic, whether this was for personal gain or otherwise, and the provision of a demon, known as a familiar (page 210), to act as an assistant. In turn, the initiate witch is alleged to have pledged allegiance to the devil and his or her soul. Pacts were often signed in public at a sabbat, but they could also be signed in a private ceremony or through the auspices of another witch.

The signing of the pact allegedly was sometimes accompanied by other rituals. These included the common one of the devil making some kind of mark, known as the devil's mark, somewhere on the body of the initiate, the mark being made in several ways, such as by the devil touching or kissing part of the body, raking his claws on it or branding it with a hot iron. Other suggested accompanying rituals included the initiate having sexual intercourse with the devil or giving him an obscene kiss (page 267), a kiss on the buttocks under his tail.

Accused witches very often confessed to having signed a pact with the devil, questions relating to this being very much a part of the standard investigation, because they had been tortured out of their minds or because they had been misled into believing that confession would save them from execution.

effigy

The use of effigies formed in the likeness of people whom witches wished to harm was allegedly common in witchcraft, and the practice can be traced back to ancient Egypt. Effigies were often made of wax, but other materials, such as clay, stuffed cloth or wood, were also used. They were sometimes called poppets, as they were in the Salem witchcraft incident.

It was thought that if a witch inflicted some damage to the effigy, a similar fate, in the form of pain, injury or even death, would affect the person whom the effigy represented. The harmful magic brought about by the creation of an effigy was supposedly made more potent by the incorporation in the effigy of some traces of the person. Thus hair, nail clippings, blood, saliva, sweat, sexual fluids, excrement, dust taken from footprints or a piece of clothing might be used in the creation of an effigy. It was because of people's fear of effigies that they were particularly careful about where they disposed of hair (page 238), nail clippings and so on.

Once the effigy had been fashioned, the witch might stick it with pins, thorns or nails to cause pain or injury in the corresponding part of the person's body. A nail through the heart, for example, was meant to cause death to the person within a short time. Alternatively, the effigy might be slowly melted or burned, sunk in water or buried. In the latter case the victims were thought to be doomed to suffer a wasting disease.

Such was the fear inspired by effigies that it was not unknown for someone to become ill at the very suggestion that one had been made of him or her. Once an image had been made, there was little a victim could do unless the witch changed her mind about inflicting harm, although it was thought that harm could sometimes be averted if the victim got hold of the effigy and buried it. The conviction that witches caused harm to their enemies by means of effigies was so strong that the possession of something that vaguely resembled an effigy was enough to bring an accusation, and even a conviction, of witchcraft.

egg

The egg was associated with witchcraft in various ways. It was popularly believed that witches could sail on the stormiest of seas by means of whole eggshells. Another popular belief was that witches could bring death to people by boiling eggs in a bucket. Eating eggs was thought to put one at risk from being influenced by witches unless the shells were thoroughly broken up after the contents had been consumed

elements

The four natural elements of earth, air, water and fire are central to modern witchcraft. They are associated with the cardinal points of the magic circle (page 265). The influence of the four elements plays an important role in the modern initiation ceremony in which the person being initiated lies on the floor within the magic circle with each of the four limbs stretched towards one of the elements.

elf-arrows

Elf-arrows were thought to be used by medieval witches to harm or kill their enemies or their enemies' livestock. These were then said to be elf-shot. This belief was particularly strong in Scotland, Ireland and Celtic parts of England, and it was thought that the skill of firing elf-arrows had been taught to witches by elves and fairies. Any unexplained decline in health could be ascribed to the victim having been elf-shot. The arrows were thought to be often invisible, but sometimes it was claimed that actual arrows had been found in the vicinity of an ill person or animal. The likeliest explanation of this is that these arrows were prehistoric arrow-shaped flints.

evil eye

This was the name given to a baleful look from a witch by which a victim might be bewitched and consequently suffer some kind of harm, injury or even death. This was associated with witchcraft but by no means restricted to it, since the concept dates back to early times and is found in cultures worldwide.

People with particularly piercing eyes were especially suspect in this respect, as were people with anything unusual about their eyes, such as having a squint or having eyes of different colours. Small children and animals were said to be at greatest risk from the evil eye. Children were often given amulets, such as red ribbons attached to their underwear or a piece of coral to wear about their persons, to protect them against this evil influence. Animals often had bells tied round their necks to protect them from the evil eye.

If amulets failed and a witch happened to cast an evil eye on (or overlooked, as this action was called) someone then some kind of counteraction had to be taken. Various incantations could be used, preferably by a white witch, but spitting, preferably spitting in the eye of the overlooker, was considered to be effective. Making a clenched fist with the thumb pushed between the index and middle fingers, known as making a fig sign, supposedly reminiscent of the devil's horns, and directing this at the suspected overlooker was also meant to counteract the evil eye.

five-fold kiss

This is a ritual of modern witchcraft involving kisses bestowed on five parts of the body, usually the feet, knees, the area above the pubic hair, the breasts and the lips. The kissing is carried out within a magic circle to the accompaniment of blessings and on a man-to-woman or woman-to-man basis.

flying ointment

This was the name given to a preparation concocted by witches to facilitate their flying on their broomsticks. They were alleged to smear it on themselves and/or on their broomsticks. The ointment was supposedly prepared according to instructions given by the devil and was alleged either to be black or dark green in colour. The ointment was said to contain, among other things, the fat of human babies who had been killed before baptism, various plants, such as belladonna and hemlock, and bat's blood.

garter

Garters were considered in traditional witch lore to be associated with the devil. Also known as pointes, garters were alleged to form part of the devil's dress.

Garters are associated with modern witchcraft but with a different purpose. They are worn in various rites as badges of rank. The garter is considered to be the ancient emblem of the high priestess.

grimoire

Also called black books, grimoires were handbooks of magic that were popular in the Middle Ages and were particularly common from the seventeenth to the early nineteenth centuries. Such handbooks gave such details as what to wear, what tools to use, what incantations to recite, descriptions on how to create magic circles, and what recipes and spells to use in the practice of magic. The purpose of them was partly to help witches improve their magic techniques, but grimoires are traditionally thought to go back to ancient times and were thought originally to have been designed with the purpose of conjuring up and controlling demons and spirits.

Much of the material for later grimoires is said to have come from the Key of Solomon, attributed to King Solomon, the biblical king who was known for his wisdom and who is said to have commanded a host of demons. *See* book of shadows, page 248.

grove

A grove is the meeting place of a group of modern witches,

usually in an outdoor setting. The name can also be used of the group itself.

hagstone

In witch lore a hagstone was a small stone with a hole in it that was hung in houses or on stable or cowshed doors or worn about the person or on animal's necks to keep witches away. Hagstones were used particularly to keep witches from borrowing horses at night to ride to sabbats and returning them in the morning exhausted and soaking with sweat. They were hung on bedsteads to keep away demons that caused nightmares.

hand of glory

This was the name given to the severed right hand of a hanged man, usually a murderer, this being supposedly rich in magic properties and therefore much valued by witches. It was thought to be at its most effective if it was cut from the corpse before it had been cut down from the gallows. Then it was wrapped in a piece of shroud, squeezed dry of blood and fluid, and pickled in an earthenware vessel with salt, long peppers and saltpetre. After two weeks it was removed from the pickling substance and laid out to dry in the sun in the so-called dog days of August or dried in an oven with vervain.

The blood and fluids that had been extracted from the hand were mixed with salt and other ingredients, reduced to a dry powder and stuffed back into the hand. Candles were then made from the fat of the murderer, the wicks of the candles often supposedly being made from the hanged man's hair. These candles were then fitted to the hand between the fingers. Another method of curing and lighting the hand involved bleeding the hand, drying it and dipping it in wax so that the fingers themselves could be lit and act as candles. Yet another method involved simply drying and pickling the hand and setting the fingers alight.

The hand of glory was reputed to be able to immobilise people and render them speechless. People breaking into houses at night supposedly used hands of glory to make sure that the occupants did not stir. It was believed that witches' brews would be particularly lethal if there was a hand of glory alight as they boiled.

horseshoe

The horseshoe is a common symbol of good luck. However, it was also regarded as providing protection against witches and other evil beings. To be used as a witch-deterrent it was hung with the ends pointed downwards, as opposed to upwards as in its use as a good luck symbol. The horseshoes were made of iron, which was regarded as a powerful witch-deterrent, and were hung on stable doors to prevent witches from borrowing horses to transport them to sabbats. If placed on the door to a house or other building the horseshoe was thought to prevent witches from crossing the threshold. If it was placed at the entrance to a chimney it was thought to prevent a witch from flying down the chimney on her broom. Tied to a bedstead it was thought to prevent the sleepers from having nightmares thought to be caused by demons. It was a condition of the anti-witch powers of horseshoes that they were never removed from the place where they had been installed. *See* horse, page 215.

image *see* EFFIGY.

knot

Witches were alleged to make use of knots in the course of their magic to aid them in the casting of effective spells. They were also said to conduct a ritual involving the tying of a knot in a length of cord, this ritual having the effect of rendering impotent the male partner in a marriage. A favourite time for witches to conduct such a ritual was on the occasion of the marriage of a man whom they particularly disliked. To counteract the spell of impotence, the bridegroom was advised to leave the shoelace in one of his shoes untied [?] as he walked up the aisle during the wedding ceremony.

If a witch wished a dying person particular harm, she supposedly tied knots on the bedclothes on the deathbed. This act reputedly prolonged the death throes of the person.

Witches were said to be able to control the winds at sea by means of cords with three knots tied in them. The untying of one knot was meant to result in a gentle southwesterly wind, the untying of the second in a strong north wind and the untying of the third in a veritable tempest. Sailors often bought these supposed wind-controllers.

Knots were also supposedly used by witches to cause death to their enemies. A string with nine knots tied in it and hidden away was meant to have the power to bring a lingering death to the intended victim. This was known as a witch's ladder.

kiss of shame *see* OBSCENE KISS.

left hand

Since Christ is traditionally depicted as sitting at God's right hand, this hand became associated with good and righteousness. Witches were popularly supposed to use their left hands more than their right hands to stir their brews and work their evil magic. They were also thought to do as many things as possible in an anticlockwise or widdershins direction, the opposite direction to which the sun passes through the heavens. When witches made their pacts with the devil as indications of their oaths of allegiance, they supposedly signed the pact in blood taken from their left hands.

All this was unfortunate for people who had more dexterity with their left hands than with their right hands. They were at risk of being accused of witchcraft or some other evil.

ligature

Ligature was the use of magic to make a man impotent. This could be done by witches by tying a knot or knots in a length of cord and keeping this hidden. The spell could not be broken unless the cord was located and the knots untied.

Another method of ligature involved the giving of potions to the hapless male. *See* knot.

magic circle

Such a circle was associated with witchcraft and was regarded as being an area within which magic could be conducted without danger of the person or people involved in the magic bringing harm to themselves. For example, it was traditionally held that witches could call up demons from within the safety of the circle. The circle, traditionally nine feet in diameter, was regarded as having the ability to enhance the magical power of the witch. Witches were strongly advised against leaving the magic circle until their magic ritual was complete on pain of possible death.

The magic circle is also used in modern witchcraft to establish a field of energy, and the altar and any tools to be used in a ritual, such as the wand, cauldron, etc, are placed within the confines of the circle. Candles are placed on the floor or ground at the four cardinal points, or quarters, and consecrated with the four elements – earth, water, air and fire.

A magic circle can sometimes also be formed as a protective force. Formerly circles might be drawn around the beds of sick people to keep away demons. Later, magic circles have been used to ward off psychic forces.

Malleus Maleficarum

Regarded as one of the most comprehensive guides to witchcraft ever published, this was more a guide to the prosecution of witches than to witchcraft itself. First published in Germany in 1486, it was compiled by Heinrich Kramer and James Sprenger with the approval of Pope Innocent VIII. They were greatly feared as part of the Inquisition, the role of which was to stamp out heresy using extremely cruel methods. At that time, particularly in Europe, witchcraft was seen as a form of heresy, so it was considered necessary to stamp it out in the same way.

The publication consisted of three parts. The first part was concerned with how the devil and his witch followers carried out a variety of evil deeds against both humans and animals. The second part was concerned with how witches cast spells and bewitched people and animals, and what could be done to prevent or undo this, and it made specific reference to witches making pacts with the devil. The third part was concerned with the legal process of trying accused witches, mentioning torture as an incentive to confession and the right of judges to make false promises of clemency to the accused to prompt confession, and it gave instructions on death sentences.

The book became phenomenally successful in Europe within a remarkably short time and became a bible for investigators and judges. Later writers used it as a basis for their own writings. It was not until 1584 that there was an English edition and the influence of the book was much more muted in England than on the continent.

obscene kiss

This was one of the names given to the kiss that witches bestowed on their master, the devil, on his buttocks underneath his tail. Also known as the kiss of shame, or *osculum infame*, such a kiss was part of the ritual at sabbats, and it is alleged that all initiates had to bestow such a kiss at their first sabbat. It was claimed that the devil often adopted an animal shape when he was receiving this particular from of allegiance.

osculum infame see OBSCENE KISS.

pentacle

The pentacle, which is a five-pointed star with a single point upright, has long been regarded as a powerful symbol in magic. It is extremely important in modern witchcraft. The pentacle is most often known as a pentagram, particularly when it is written or drawn. It is the witch's symbol of positive force and is also a symbol associated with protection.

The pentacle, in the form of a clay, earthenware or wax disc inscribed with a pentagram and other symbols, is used to consecrate the magic circle.

Traditionally the pentacle, as well as increasing the magic powers of magicians, witches, etc, was thought to be a protector against witchcraft and other forms of evil. Pentagrams were, therefore, frequently drawn on doors in order to prevent witches or evil spirits from entering.

pentagram *see* PENTACLE.

pin

Pins were alleged to play various roles in witchcraft. Witches supposedly used them in the pursuit of their magic, and people were advised always to pick up any dropped pins to prevent witches from using these in the casting of their spells. Pins were also used by anyone who had fashioned an effigy of an enemy and wished to harm that person, the pins being stuck into various parts of the effigy's anatomy in the hope that this would cause pain in a corresponding part of the person and might even lead to death.

Witches were also accused of using pins to make various curses. One of these involved the taking of a lemon, uttering various incantations over this and sticking it with various pins, including several black ones.

Pins were used in witchcraft trials in the search for any trace of the devil's mark (page 254), the finding of which was held to represent evidence of witchcraft. In the test for witchcraft known as pricking (page 75) pins, bodkins or other sharp objects were jabbed into the skin of witches in the hope of locating an insensitive area or an area that did not bleed and so supposedly proving an association with the devil.

People who were supposedly in the grips of demonic possession (page 275) often supposedly vomited up pins along with other objects.

poppet *see* EFFIGY.

scissors

Scissors were thought to offer protection against witches and other evil beings. It was advised that if a pair of scissors was left under the threshold of a house or under a doormat then no witch would dare seek entrance, particularly if the scissors were left in an open position, thereby making a shape approximating that of the cross.

tears

According to tradition witches could not shed tears, which were meant to be an offence to the devil. If an accused witch did not weep in the course of the pain caused by testing and torturing, it was assumed by the investigators that she could not weep and therefore must be a witch. No recognition was given to the fact that the accused witch might be in too much shock to cry and that in any case tears are more often a response to emotional trauma than to physical pain.

If an accused witch was found weeping privately in her cell this was not an advantage to her. It was simply assumed that this was a deception inspired by the devil. It was also alleged that witches smeared their faces with spittle in order to fake tears on their cheeks.

wand

The wand, the concept of which goes back to prehistoric times, was the allegedly magic stick that witches used in the casting of their spells and in the invocation of spirits. It was alleged that witches were given wands by the devil at the time of their initiation. The wand could be made of various materials. Most usual was the wood from the hazel tree but wood from the willow was also common, it being considered best to cut the wood when the moon was full or waxing.

wart

The archetypal witch is depicted as being an ugly old woman, and in England especially it is the case that many people who were accused of witchcraft were in fact simply unattractive, eccentric old women. The stereotypical image of the witch often involves a wart, which adds to the ugliness. In fact if a person was accused of being a witch it was particularly if she had a wart somewhere on her body, especially one on a hidden part of the body. It was highly likely that a zealous investigator searching for supposed evidence of witchcraft would designate such a wart as a witch's mark (page 273).

It was important for people to avoid getting warts and to get rid of them if they had them. One way to avoid getting warts was supposedly to avoid handling toads. There were various traditional ways of getting rid of warts. One of these also involved toads, but it was most unfortunate for the toad concerned. The sufferer from warts was urged to carry a toad around in a bag worn around the neck until the creature died. Other less dramatic ways included tying a piece of silk around the offending wart or spitting on it every morning. These are only a few suggested remedies because getting rid of warts seems once to have been a major preoccupation.

witch ball

A glass ball, originally about seven inches in diameter, once hung in windows as a witch-deterrent and was then used as a decoration. Many were mainly blue or green in colour, and some were made of reflective glass to act as convex mirrors. Witch balls were popular in England from the eighteenth century onwards.

witch bottle

A witch bottle was used to counteract any evil spells that might have been cast by witches. It consisted of a glass, iron or bellarmine bottle or flask into which went some of the victim's urine and often also a piece of hair and some nail clippings. There are various traditions as to what happened to the bottle after that.

One indicates that the witch bottle was buried, causing the spell to be lifted and also causing the witch who had cast the spell to suffer great pain or discomfort. Another suggests that the witch bottle was put on the hearth at midnight and left to boil. This supposedly resulted in great pain being inflicted on the caster of the spell, causing her to lift the spell. Alternatively, the witch might be drawn to the scene of the boiling and thus cause herself to be identified. Yet another tradition has it that the bottle of urine was thrown on the fire and when it exploded the spell was broken and the witch killed.

Some suggest that there was originally quite a ceremony associated with the witch bottle when the idea first came into being. According to this suggestion, the heating of the bottle was accompanied by the saying of the Lord's Prayer backwards. Such a recitation was traditionally associated with witchcraft, and it was supposedly the case that the combination of the urine-boiling and the recitation would remove the spell from the victim and also make it applicable to the person who had cast it.

The custom of making witch bottles is said to have been introduced to England from Holland. It became popular in parts of England, particularly in East Anglia where there was a strong belief in witchcraft and where the custom is said to have survived for some considerable time.

witch box

A witch box contained things that were meant to protect the inhabitants of a house from the evils of witchcraft. Witch boxes were common in England in the sixteenth and seventeenth centuries and consisted of small wooden boxes with glass fronts. They might contain, for example, a sprig of rowan, or of any other tree or plant that was thought to act as a protection against witchcraft, a paper with some holy words written on it, a cross and anything else that was regarded as being a witch-deterrent. Sometimes a magic spell of protection was cast over the box. Selling such boxes was one of the ways in which witch-finders made money when zealously going from town to town seeking out witches to accuse and charge.

witch's hat

In modern depictions of traditional witches they are almost always wearing tall, pointed hats with broad brims. These are as an essential part of the witch stereotype as a broomstick and yet early descriptions of witches do not indicate any special headwear for them. In medieval woodcuts witches do not appear wearing pointed hats but either have flowing hair or are wearing whatever form of headwear was popular at the time.

There are various theories as to why the wide-brimmed pointed hat has become associated with witchcraft. The most popular one is that such a hat is an adaptation of the hat commonly worn by Puritan women in England in the early seventeenth century. These were blunt-topped but otherwise bore a resemblance to the stereotypical witch's hat.

It was during this period that witchcraft hysteria in England was at its worst. It has been suggested that the move from the blunt top to the pointed top as far as witches were concerned was because the top of the pointed hat was thought to represent one of the devil's horns.

Another suggested reason for the witch's hat is that it is an adaptation of the brimless, conical cap. The theory is that perhaps an artist at some point added a broad brim to this in the belief that this addition made the cap more suitable for women.

The pointed hats play no part in the rituals of modern witches. Most wear nothing on their heads, although some wear headbands decorated with a crescent moon or other symbol placed on the forehead.

witch's ladder *see* KNOT.

witch's mark

This took the form of a protuberance on the skin, or occasionally an extra nipple. In fact such a mark was probably a wart, mole, a birthmark or simply a raised spot or bump. To the witch investigator such a protuberance was evidence of witchcraft as it was taken to be the site where a witch suckled her familiar (page 210), it being a popular belief that a witch rewarded her familiar by letting it suck a few drops of her blood. Protuberances that secreted either blood or other fluid, or even those that were red in colour, were thought to be particularly suspect.

As with the search for the devil's mark (page 254), the investigators searching for a witch's mark were exceptionally zealous. Exceptional attention was made to the hidden areas of the body, such as under the tongue or in the folds of the vagina. Almost anything could be judged to be such a mark, and many an innocent person was convicted on the grounds of bearing what were undoubtedly innocent marks. The search for a witch's mark was a major part of witchcraft trials in England and Scotland and later in New England.

Acts and Actions

dancing

Dancing played a large part in the festivities enjoyed by witches at their sabbats. Much of the dancing was said to be of an indecent or obscene nature, and it is claimed that the witch dancers were often naked. It is said that it was traditional for the dancing of the witches to get faster and faster until the dancers went into a frenzy and committed all manner of sexual acts. The devil allegedly was often present on such occasions and at least some of the dancing witches supposedly had sexual intercourse with him.

Modern witchcraft also has a dancing element as part of its rituals, but this is totally unlike that allegedly present in sabbats. A circle dance known as the Dance of the Wheel is performed in celebration of the winter solstice.

demonic possession

The idea of people being taken over by demons is an ancient one and by no means restricted to its association with witchcraft. With reference to witchcraft it was believed that witches could introduce demons into people so that they were completely taken over and began behaving and speaking very strangely. Witches allegedly often introduced demons into their victims by means of innocent-looking food, such as apples.

Allegedly, once the demon was introduced the victim might be affected in a number of different ways. Some would go into fits, faint regularly or seem to be attacked by bouts of severe pain, and some would behave wildly, very loudly and often obscenely. Alterations were supposedly often spotted, and some supposed victims allegedly seemed to undergo physical changes and even change their shape radically. It was claimed that some had gross distended bellies and would from time to time vomit up strange objects such as pins. Others, it was claimed, seemed to suffer from a wasting disease. Voices allegedly often changed completely, often becoming much deeper and gruffer than was usually the case.

There are almost certainly several rational explanations of the supposed demonic possessions that were so widespread at the height of the witchcraft trials. Some of the people who were supposedly possessed by demons were very likely suffering from a variety of mental illnesses while those who simply had seizures may well have been suffering from epilepsy. Others very probably decided to act in the way in which they had heard possessed people acted in order to draw attention to themselves, and in this they usually succeeded. They could add to this attention by naming a particular witch or witches.

One person faking the antics of the possessed in order to draw attention to himself or herself often had a knock-on effect. Others would also indulge in such behaviour, perhaps in what would be known today as a copycat exercise and perhaps as a hysterical reaction. There seems little doubt that in the relatively closed communities, such as nunneries or small towns, that were affected by supposed demonic possession, there was at least an element of hysteria. One person would start behaving wildly and others would follow suit, carried away by the whole thing and perhaps wanting to share in the attention. It is possible that some people faked demonic possession and named a specific person as the cause simply out of vengeance for some supposed ill. Where nuns or young women were involved it is thought that repressed sexual desire might have been a factor.

It must often have been obvious that there was something decidedly suspect going on when demonic possession, especially mass demonic possession, was claimed. However, at the height of the witchcraft hysteria the investigators were more intent on proving accused witches guilty than on finding them innocent. Therefore many cases of supposed demonic possession were not looked into very carefully.

The most popular cure for demonic possession was exorcism. This involved a priest ordering the demons to depart and sometimes the use of holy water and prayer. Often the exorcist tried to identify the demon or demons by name, supposedly indulged in arguments with him or them and issued threats. Exorcism, often conducted publicly, was repeated until the demons were gone. In cases where the supposed demonic possession was the result of a desire for attention or a need for revenge, the public exorcism often effected a cure since there was once again attention on them.

drawing down the moon

This is a ritual of modern witchcraft. In this ceremony the high priestess of a coven goes into a trance, reciting a poetic address that is sometimes spontaneous. By this process she becomes the goddess, symbolised by the moon.

elf-shooting *see* ELF-ARROW.

exorcism *see* DEMONIC POSSESSION.

flying *see* BROOMSTICK.

grave-robbing

According to tradition, witches often used human remains in the casting of their spells and in the making of their brews. Thus they were accused of desecrating graves and removing parts of the corpses. They allegedly were particularly anxious to obtain parts of the corpses of those who died young in a violent way, and people who had met their deaths on the gallows were of especial interest to them. Supposedly witches sometimes bribed executioners into parting with the corpses or parts of the corpses of those whom they had put to death. Of even more interest than the corpses of the hanged, it was claimed, were the corpses of babies who had died before the ceremony of baptism could take place.

hand-fasting

In modern witchcraft the rite corresponding to marriage is known as hand-fasting. The ceremony takes place within a magic circle and is officiated over by the high priest and high priestess of the relevant coven. The union effected by hand-fasting is not designated to be lifelong but to last as long as love lasts. In some ceremonies the couple taking part in the ceremony leap over a broomstick in the expectation that this will bring them luck.

initiation

Certain traditions are associated with the initiation of witches, although these varied from period to period, place to place and tradition to tradition. Some of the alleged rituals associated with initiation included the signing of the devil's pact (page 255), the marking by the Devil of the initiate in some way, thereby imposing what was known as the devil's mark (page 254), and the bestowing by the initiate of an obscene kiss (page 267) on the devil's buttocks.

The new witch, it was alleged, sometimes underwent a travesty of the Christian baptismal ceremony and was given a new name. Sometimes the initiate was rewarded with a familiar (page 210) and some of the tools of her new trade, such as a broomstick and some flying ointment (page 260). In some cases it was claimed that the new witch was required to have sexual intercourse with her master, the devil.

lycanthropy

This refers to the supposed transformation of a human being into a wolf. *See* werewolf, page 221.

maleficia

This referred to the evil or harmful deeds that witches supposedly carried out. There were a whole range of these, and they included injuring or killing people or livestock by bewitching them, the making of an effigy (page 257), again with the purpose of injuring or killing someone, or overlooking someone, that is, using the evil eye (page 259). Turning milk sour, turning butter rancid, spoiling beer as it brewed, making hens cease to lay or cows cease to give milk or damaging crops were among the least of their supposed bad deeds. Storm-raising (page 280) was another deed of which witches were often accused.

metamorphosis *see* SHAPE-CHANGING.

overlooking *see* EVIL EYE.

possession *see* DEMONIC POSSESSION.

scrying

Witches were credited with the ability to divine the future by concentrating on something with a shiny, reflective surface, such as a mirror or a crystal ball. This was sometimes known as scrying.

sending

This referred to the sending of creatures, such as animals or birds, to effect a piece of magic or to carry out a curse rather than the person behind the magic or curse going in person and being identified. In the case of witchcraft the creature involved was alleged to be her familiar (page 210).

shape-shifting, shape-changing

It was widely believed that witches were capable of changing their physical form. This they supposedly did so that they could perform their evil deeds without being spotted. The transformation or metamorphosis was allegedly often brought about by the smearing on the body of a magic ointment, sometimes given by the devil and sometimes made by themselves, and the performing of a magic ritual.

When witches changed shape they allegedly often adopted the shape of an animal, especially cats, dogs or hares, but there was a wide choice. The belief that they could change shape was often not to the advantage of witches. This was because any cat, dog, hare or other creature seen around the village or town at some scene of disaster could very easily be claimed to be an accused witch in disguise and indeed this could be the sole basis of a charge of witchcraft.

storm-raising

Among the activities most popularly associated with witchcraft was storm-raising, an activity that might be indulged in both by witches who lived by the sea and those who lived inland. The coastal witches were wont to raise tempests in order to cause wrecks at sea while their inland equivalents were more inclined to raise storms in order to destroy crops and buildings and to injure or kill people.

Allegedly there were several ways in which witches could

storm-raise. For example, they were thought to throw the contents of their cauldrons into the sea after a sabbat (page 286) to work up a fierce storm. They were credited with the ability to throw bolts of lightning as they flew on their broomsticks whether over sea or land. It was alleged that they could raise rain storms by sacrificing cocks in cauldrons or by digging holes and either pouring water into these or urinating in them.

At the time of the witchcraft hysteria people were much more reliant on weather than was the case in later times. Communities were very much agriculture-based, and if anything happened to the crops it was a disaster for the whole community. Often scapegoats were sought in the face of such natural disaster and at the times of the witchcraft trials villagers looked around for a likely person to accuse of witchcraft and storm-raising. *See* knot, page 264.

transvection

This refers to the alleged transportation through the air of witches, usually on broomsticks. *See* broomstick, page 249.

Words

charm

We are more used nowadays to regarding charms as objects that bring luck. Originally, however, they were words, phrases or chants spoken in connection with magic. With reference to witchcraft, charms were used both by witches and by those wishing to protect themselves against witchcraft.

Witches allegedly chanted charms over their brews or over their tools to make these more effective and also chanted them over effigies for the same purpose. Others might recite a charm before they retired for the night or chant one over someone who was ill in order to keep witchcraft at bay. Certain charms were thought to be effective in curing ailments.

Some charms were written down on parchment, paper or wood and carried about the person. These were the forerunners of charms as we know them. Modern witchcraft uses the concept of the spoken charm but modern witches do not refer to the word as such, preferring such terms as chanting or incantation.

hex

A hex, meaning a curse or malevolent spell, is a term that ultimately derives from the German *Hexe*, a witch. Hex was a common term in the American colonies and was brought there by the Pennsylvanian Dutch who had borrowed the term from German. People who wished to harm other people or get revenge on them for some reason would consult someone thought to be a witch in order to get hexes placed on their enemies. There were also people who claimed to specialise in removing such hexes, and these might be consulted by those who were experiencing a period of particular misfortune and were of the opinion that a hex might be at the root of this

night spell

This was not a spell cast by a witch but a set recitation said at night before going to sleep that was intended to keep the sleeper free from the activities of witches or other evil beings while he or she was asleep.

Gatherings and Groups

black mass

The black mass is depicted as being a travesty of the holy mass held in Catholic churches. In fact the black mass is more a feature of Satanism than witchcraft, and modern witches do not indulge in this, since they do not worship the devil. There is little evidence that old-style witchcraft was associated with black masses and few confessions of witchcraft are thought to refer to them. Some confessions might include some details connected with the concept of the black mass, such as desecration of the host, the defilement of the cross or saying the Lord's Prayer backwards, but there is no evidence that there was a single established rite. The connection between witchcraft and the black mass, however, is one that appealed to writers of novels and film scripts and so the two are now linked in people's minds.

coven

Coven was the name traditionally given to a group of witches who allegedly met together on a regular basis, the word being probably linked to the verb 'convene'. The concept of witches' covens dates back to the twelfth century but the concept did not come into its own until the witchcraft trials of the Renaissance period.

It suited those who were convinced that witches existed and who were determined to get rid of them to think of them as meeting in subversive groups to plot harm. This increased people's fear of witchcraft and also gave great scope for witches who had confessed to have supposed evidence for naming names of others. It was one of the features of witch-craft trials that those who were accused and either voluntarily or involuntarily confessed identified others whom they claimed were also involved in witchcraft. Claiming that one had attended a coven with several others made such claims appear more plausible.

Whether there existed such an organisation as a coven is at best open to debate. In England at least the archetypal witch was a solitary old woman of unattractive appearance and ec-centric habits who laid claim to healing powers and a sup-posed gift of clairvoyance. Such a person seems very unlikely to have belonged to an organised coven. The British anthro-pologist Margaret Murray (*see* page 13) did much to foster the idea that covens were prevalent and also the idea that they consisted of thirteen people, this probably based on the idea of Christ and the twelve apostles, in the case of witchcraft the devil substituting for Christ. This has been much disputed, however, and there is little evidence to support the theory.

The British popular concept of a witch was of a strange old woman living alone except for a cat or other pet, taken to be her familiar (page 210). It seems unlikely that such a person would belong to a structured group but it often suited the au-thorities to believe this.

The coven is part of the organisation of modern witchcraft,

each coven being an independent unit. There are few statistics relating to these as many prefer to practise witchcraft without drawing attention either to themselves or to the groups to which they belong. It would be difficult to keep count as practically any professed witch can start a coven. Each coven screens anyone who expresses a desire to join and each is thought to have its own book of shadows (page 248).

The coven meets regularly, such a meeting being known as an esbat. Such meetings may take place either outdoors or inside and usually take place thirteen times a year on the occasion of the full moon. However, it depends on the individual coven how often they choose to meet and some meet much more frequently.

Members of a coven are known as coveners and are led by the high priestess, representing the goddess (page 212), sometimes sharing the leadership with a high priest, representing the horned god (page 215). The traditional number in a modern coven is thirteen, but this is far from being rigid and the number can vary from around three to twenty.

grove *see* **GROVE.**

Hallowe'en

Hallowe'en, celebrated on 31 October, occurs on the eve of All Soul's Day and is the equivalent of the Celtic festival of Samhain, associated with fire and death. Hallowe'en is the festival most associated with witchcraft, it being an occasion when ghosts and demons are said to walk the earth, and allegedly it was the occasion of one of the major sabbats.

The festival is celebrated by children, and often now by

grownups, by attending fancy-dress parties dressed as witches, ghosts, etc, and by making lanterns out of turnips or pumpkins. In Scotland the children go 'guising', that is, they disguise themselves in fancy-dress costumes and go around local houses performing some kind of act of entertainment and receiving in return small gifts, such as apples or sweets, and various traditional games are played. These customs are now being confused with the American custom of trick or treat, when children go round the houses asking for sweets or other treats in exchange for not doing any harm to the householders.

sabbat

A sabbat allegedly was a celebratory gathering of witches involving feasting, drinking, wild naked dancing and abandoned sexual activity reminiscent of old pagan rites. The word was first mentioned in relation to a witchcraft trial in Toulouse in France in 1335 but it was not commonly used until the middle of the fifteenth century. In England the term was much later, around 1620.

The sabbat was essentially a tribute to the master of the witches, the devil, who was usually present, and it was alleged that he would have sexual intercourse with at least some of the witches present. Sabbats were supposed to take place at infrequent but regular intervals and to attract a large attendance. Witches traditionally flew to them on their broomsticks. Sabbats were thought to be night-time occasions, breaking up when the cock crew and signalled dawn.

Various activities, other than the feasting, drinking, wild dancing and lewd sexual behaviour, allegedly took place at sabbats. Particularly in Europe it was thought that sabbats were occasions when the black mass (page 283) was held, this being a heretical parody of the Catholic mass. The sabbat was allegedly a favourite occasion for initiation (page 278) ceremonies, with much signing of the devil's pact (page 255), etc. It was also supposedly one of the few occasions on which the devil met his followers en masse and the latter indulged in the practice of bestowing on him the obscene kiss (page 267), a kiss on his buttocks. Sabbat activities, it was claimed, might involve the witches reciting to the devil catalogues of the evil deeds that they had carried out since the previous sabbat. A particularly macabre aspect of the sabbat is that it was associated with the sacrifice, cooking and eating of unbaptised infants.

It suited witch-finders very well to spread belief in sabbats. Questions about them were part of the standard inquisition of accused witches to elicit confessions. A confession that included attendance at a sabbat, at which hundreds or even thousands or other witches, might allegedly have been present, gave immense scope for other people being named. It was a feature of witchcraft trials that when people confessed, often after considerable pressure and torture, the self-confessed witches named other people as witches also.

Modern witchcraft retains the concept of the sabbat but such gatherings have nothing to do with the devil, involving feasting and dancing without the lewd diabolical rites. They are held regularly, often at times of old pagan seasonal festivals held to celebrate the changing of the seasons.

Walpurgisnacht

According to the German witchcraft tradition, Walpurgisnacht, celebrated on 30 April and the occasion of the Celtic

Witchcraft

celebration of Beltane Eve, was the occasion of one of the major witch sabbats. Witches throughout Germany, Holland and Scandinavia supposedly held such a sabbat on mountain tops and indulged in the usual rituals and orgies thought to be a regular part of sabbats.

Modern witches tend to celebrate this date also with feasting, dancing and rituals but there is no connection between such celebration and the devil or demons. It is more a recognition and celebration of the changing seasons.